WHERE THE HEART IS

www.penguin.co.uk

Where the Heart Is

*Eight Ways to Transform Your
Life at Home, No Matter
Where You Live*

KATIE McCRORY

torva

TRANSWORLD PUBLISHERS

UK | USA | Canada | Ireland | Australia
India | New Zealand | South Africa

Transworld is part of the Penguin Random House group of companies whose addresses can be found at global.penguinrandomhouse.com.

Penguin Random House UK, One Embassy Gardens,
8 Viaduct Gardens, London SW11 7BW

penguin.co.uk

First published in Great Britain in 2026 by Torva
an imprint of Transworld Publishers

001

Copyright © Katie McCrory 2026

The moral right of the author has been asserted

Words from 'Don't Hesitate' by Mary Oliver reprinted by the permission of The Charlotte Sheedy Literary Agency as agent for the author. Copyright © 2010, 2017 by Mary Oliver with permission of Bill Reichblum.

Every effort has been made to obtain the necessary permissions with reference to copyright material, both illustrative and quoted. We apologize for any omissions in this respect and will be pleased to make the appropriate acknowledgements in any future edition.

Penguin Random House values and supports copyright. Copyright fuels creativity, encourages diverse voices, promotes freedom of expression and supports a vibrant culture. Thank you for purchasing an authorized edition of this book and for respecting intellectual property laws by not reproducing, scanning or distributing any part of it by any means without permission. You are supporting authors and enabling Penguin Random House to continue to publish books for everyone. No part of this book may be used or reproduced in any manner for the purpose of training artificial intelligence technologies or systems. In accordance with Article 4(3) of the DSM Directive 2019/790, Penguin Random House expressly reserves this work from the text and data mining exception.

Typeset in 12/15.5pt Minion Pro by Six Red Marbles UK, Thetford, Norfolk
Printed and bound in Great Britain by Clays Ltd, Elcograf S.p.A.

The authorized representative in the EEA is Penguin Random House Ireland, Morrison Chambers, 32 Nassau Street, Dublin D02 YH68.

A CIP catalogue record for this book is available from the British Library

ISBN: 9781911709831

Penguin Random House is committed to a sustainable future for our business, our readers and our planet. This book is made from Forest Stewardship Council® certified paper.

For James, Órla and Rufus – I love coming home to you all.

Contents

Introduction		1
1	Comfort	15
2	Control	43
3	Security	68
4	Accomplishment	95
5	Belonging	121
6	Nurturing	152
7	Joy	177
8	Aspiration	204
Conclusion: A Never-ending Story		229
Acknowledgements		239
Resources		243
Endnotes		251

Introduction

'Home is a place we all must find, child. It's not just a place where you eat or sleep. Home is knowing. Knowing your mind, knowing your heart, knowing your courage. If we know ourselves, we're always home, anywhere.'

Glinda the Good, The Wiz

When I was twenty-three years old, I lived with a woman who didn't know how to close the front door. At least once a week, I'd come home to find it swinging open on its hinges, our furniture and electronics miraculously unrobbed. We were five housemates in total, living across three floors in a terraced house on a residential side street in Brixton, South London. The first time I met everyone was the day I moved in. Initially, the persistent open door was a mystery to us all. The first time it happened, Joey, my Italian-American housemate (yes, really), came storming into the living room to gently rebuke one of us 'dipshitted assholes' for leaving us open to murder and theft. He had a point. And yet it continued.

We were already a paranoid bunch, taking our

own toilet roll into the bathroom and labelling our cheese. For weeks, I had an argument sustained entirely via Post-it notes about where the laundry basket was supposed to live. In this humming dystopia, the door became an irresistible fixation that defied common sense or comprehension. The more we contrived to crack open the truth from one another, the more we wound each other up.

It's so easy to live with someone and never talk to them. In the absence of conversation, all we had to go on was action, or inaction. The landlord suggested a weekly Residents' Meeting, which we squirmed through for a month or so until we each found reasons to be busy. I didn't need an excuse; I scarcely touched the sides of that home. My life had just been shaken up and London was fizzing through my veins. I was newly single and finally employed in a Proper Job that paid so badly it didn't even hit the lowest UK tax threshold, but it knocked me into a social circle that filled my glass and kept me out until 3 a.m. four nights a week. I didn't have time for a domestic life, and I certainly didn't have time to make friends with my housemates.

As the weeks peeled by, and the door continued to exist beyond the realm of handles or locks, we asked the landlord to install an alarm. It would, we reasoned, be impossible to set the alarm and leave the door open or open the door without setting the alarm off. The very nature of having an alarm made us newly alert to who was in the house and when, because you could only set it when we were all out. Well, that was fine, we concluded; we just had to establish when everyone left for work in the morning, and the last person out would put it on. The landlord, ever-inclined to officialdom, called an Extraordinary Residents' Meeting and we gathered around the table for what we all silently prayed would be our last enforced meal together.

That was when we found out that the most inoffensive of our flatmates, a young woman called Olivia who I had barely registered as living there, had lost her job. A few months back, actually. She was struggling to find something new and so she'd taken up baking in the meantime. She'd made some brownies for us. They had something special in them too . . . Did we want one? Everything started to make a lot more sense after I realized that Olivia had been high every single day since I'd first met her. She appeared to be newly surprised about the door that evening, as if receiving this remarkable information for the very first time. She giggled her way through the rest of the meeting until we all traipsed up to bed, exhausted by the emotional toll of living with people you cannot wrap your head around. When I came back down for a glass of water, Olivia had dragged her duvet and pillow downstairs. She was making a nest just behind the front door, promising to stay alert all night in the hopes of catching the moment when the door magically sprang open on its hinges. I didn't know whether to laugh or cry.

By that time in my life, I had moved home seventeen times. In fact, the day I walked through the perennially open front door of my new home in Brixton, I had moved four times between two countries in six months. I would go on to move another eight or so times, and on to another country. It wasn't until I moved into the home where I live today – the place where I have lived almost the longest – that I actually asked myself what I needed and wanted from it.

When I look back at the various places I've called home over the last four decades, I see refracted images of myself, as if each act of homemaking revealed a new facet of my identity. Moving home, through choice or through circumstance, is how I have moved through life. Sometimes I moved with a rucksack; other times I took a lorryful of packing boxes and bubble-wrapped valuables. But how many of those front doors opened into places that actually *felt* like home? Half, maybe? Less, to be honest. I have come to learn, often the hard way, that where we live and where we feel at home can be very different places. This book is about what makes that difference.

Today I live in a small apartment in Copenhagen, the Danish capital that's home to beers, bikes and statuesque blondes. I moved here with my husband in 2015, during a heatwave. Those first weeks in the city were spent in a spritz-fuelled haze as the long summer days melted into ambient warm nights, and we did little more than bounce between the bars and cafes that lined the historic canals and cobbled streets. When I filed the papers for my residency card and was asked to give the reason for my relocation, there was no box for me to tick. I had no permanent job, no studies, no family already living here to reunite with. After years of battling with London, we had quite simply moved for life, and Copenhagen appeared to be where I was best suited for living it. Even the inevitable Scandinavian winter couldn't diminish the joy with which I embraced my new *hygge* lifestyle. I lit a lot of candles, consumed vast quantities of bread and pastries, and gleefully persisted in ordering glasses of red wine in local dive bars that only served beer on tap. I may have looked like a hobbit in a land of elves, but there was no better way to describe it: Copenhagen felt like home.

Moving to Denmark also pushed my journey home directly into the roaring freeway of my work. In late 2016 I joined the southern-Sweden-based global headquarters for an iconic and historic home-furnishing brand, and in 2017 I started leading an in-depth research study into the way that people live around the world: the IKEA *Life at Home* Report. The report has since grown to become one of the largest and most distinctive research projects of its kind in the world. At the last count, more than 37,000 people in thirty-eight countries were involved in it.

As I quickly started to learn, this sort of research is a lively blend of data, insights and poetic world-building. As well as your eyes and ears, you have to come at it with your heart and guts. I can still picture the room I was in when a wide-ranging conversation with Professor Alison Blunt, the founding co-director of the Centre for Studies of Home, landed on the ideal qualities of a home. My team and I were interviewing her as part of an expert review of the research for the 2018 report, and she was – without doubt – one of the most generous thinkers on the topic of home-making I've had the opportunity to meet. 'When thinking about the ideals of home, at the core are comfort, security, a sense of autonomy and ownership, and the capacity for privacy. But again, each of those can be challenged; they can be non-existent even in the context of the home.' She took a moment, before elaborating: 'Home at its core goes back to a sense of belonging; a sense of belonging personally and belonging collectively.'

You could feel the charge of electricity between us all as the collective light bulb went on. I'm slightly ashamed to admit that, until that moment, I didn't think I had permission to talk about home in such an emotional way, as if the temperament of homemaking was too fluffy for research or I'd fog up the insights with all my womanly feels. I was expecting her to talk about room size or lighting or something else entirely functional that you can quantify and optimize, because anything 'ideal' always seems to have a number next to it. It was like she cracked open the chest cavity of home in that room and pulled out the warm and bloody emotional needs that are the beating heart of its existence. It took a whole-hearted person to help us see that this fistful of pulsing emotions are what people mean when they talk about the 'feeling of home'. I could immediately see what kind of game-changer this was going to be.

From that point on, everything started with a simple, open question:

What does home *feel* like?

I've asked it countless times now, and what I have heard and learned in response has changed my life.

Over the coming chapters, we'll explore together what home feels like, but I want to start by telling you this: one in three people globally say they feel more at home in places other than where they live. When I heard that data-point for the first time, I shuddered at the thought of just how many people around the world feel sad, lonely, anxious, insecure or generally out of place in their own home – *their own home*! Then came a curdling feeling in my stomach, like a memory gone sour, when I realized that I have been that one in three more times than I care to remember.

What this book will demonstrate is that all of us have the opportunity to feel at home where we live – no matter the space and place we occupy, or the people and things we have around us. It's an opportunity that transcends the trends, norms and stipulations that come with different cultures, identities and backgrounds, whether you live in a single studio apartment with *tatami* mats in Tokyo, a concrete social-housing estate in Berlin or a Tudorbethan mansion in Essex. Sure, you'll always find some curious variations between countries and regions when it comes to home habits and attitudes – like, the country that's most likely to stay on top of household chores (Hungary), the one that prioritizes sleep as a way to relax (Finland), and the one that gets the most joy from watching their pets sleep (America) – but I often find that whilst we're giggling at different national caricatures, we're distracted from what's going on at a deeper level. The simple fact of the matter is that 8 billion people are all reaching for the same thing – to feel at home.

To view your own life through the lens of a research study can reveal many things if you are ready to see them. Not least the tell-tale signs of people, just like you, quietly living in spaces and places that might meet their functional needs but fail to meet their emotional ones. As the research progresses each year, wherever the team goes and whoever we meet, we always come back to the same clutch of profound feelings that people talk about time and again when we ask about their home. They talk about comfort and security; about connection and belonging. They talk about the give and take that passes between people and place, in which our entire sense of self takes root. In the early days, I would often joke that our research pursuit was as complex as trying to find out what love feels like, until it stopped feeling like a joke. Perhaps my own reckoning was inevitable, through the unpacking of the literal and metaphorical baggage that accompanied me to Scandinavia. The truth of the matter was there all along: the feeling of home *is* the feeling of love.

The hard truth is that homes have been failing us for years, chipping away at our existence by doing just enough but never more. I know what this *looks* like from the research, and I know what this *feels* like from experience. I can't help but think that you, too, know what this feels like. We're so habituated to this kind of living, we've stopped expecting better. We twist our needs and expectations to fit whatever space we're in, no matter how miserable it makes us, and try to get on with life. If a friend confided in you that their partner made them feel that way, you would tell them to end the relationship. Immediately.

This realization has led to my complete reappraisal of the notion of home and the role it has played in my life. Turning the question about what home feels like on myself forced a necessary, if painful, re-evaluation of all the homes I have lived in so far. Once I'd started, I couldn't stop this imaginary road trip. I was fired up with insights that pulsed through my core memories of homemaking, like I'd become fluent in a new language. And then two enormous events occurred in my life at the same time: I became a mother as the world dropped to its knees with Covid-19. My life at home was just about braced for the impact of a baby, but there was nothing in the parenting manuals about how to prepare for a pandemic. It suddenly became abundantly clear that our 90-square-metre apartment would be weathering an almighty storm.

As the weeks trudged by under national lockdown in Denmark, my home seemed to oscillate between a sanctuary and a prison. It was the safest place to be, but I was also its captive. During those crushingly weary night feeds, as my daughter guzzled at my breast before dawn, I felt like someone was tipping sand over me and that I might suffocate. I developed a clawing need to run out of the apartment, down the road and into green space and air and light and community. I longed to go for a coffee at my local cafe, rummage through bric-a-brac at the charity shop, or hug a friend and weep with that delirious mix of shattering love and exhaustion that accompanies early motherhood. And yet, after every daily constitutional, when my husband and I wheeled our screaming baby around the same empty neighbourhood for an hour, there was nothing more soothing than opening our front door and feeling the warm embrace of home.

I know from the research we conducted that year that I was not alone in those feelings. Four in five people said they felt their home was their sanctuary during that first year of the pandemic – but that still left one in five who didn't feel that way. We also saw that people who made changes to their home to better meet their needs were more likely to say they had improved mental health and well-being than those who didn't. At the heart of these insights, and many more besides, is a persistent gap between the emotional needs we believe it's important for our homes to fulfil and the reality of whether we get them where we live. It's this distance between what many of us want and what we actually have at home – something I call the 'emotional gap' – that holds countless untold stories about lives that are deserving of so much more. Like the people who rent a room in a house-share, for example, who are the most likely to say that they don't get *any* of their emotional needs met at home; or parents with young kids, who are the most likely to say they don't feel a sense of belonging where they live. Above all, when your relationship with home doesn't feel great – when your health and well-being is taking a hit and you just don't feel like yourself – it's almost impossible to thrive in any other area of your life.

Myriad stories and over ten years of research have given me an extraordinary front-row seat to life at home around the world and what makes it feel better. It's how my team and I at IKEA have come to name eight universal emotional needs that when fulfilled in combination create what we all call the 'feeling of home': **Comfort, Control, Security, Accomplishment, Belonging, Nurturing, Joy and Aspiration.** Knowing more about these emotional needs gives us the power and potential to transform our relationship with home. And when our life at home improves, it creates the preconditions for positive change in the rest of our life, too.

Perhaps – if we're honest – there's been a bit of a collective blind spot when it comes to acknowledging the enormous potential of the home. I can't quite shake the feeling that there's a long-standing bias against things that feel inherently 'domestic' or 'feminine' unless it can generate money or someone invents an app for it. But when we do the work to redefine our home from being a static place where we live to a dynamic place that we love, we have the chance to release endless goodness into our daily lives. There's no app for that.

If the language of home is twinned with love, then maybe we can find our way to happiness and harmony in much the same way we would with our romantic and life partners – by sharing, showing and taking care, being authentic, brave and vulnerable, having fun and exploring life together. Just talking about it this way already puts us in a completely different headspace when we think about home, right? So, what might happen if we approach our home life with as much purpose and intention as we approach our love life? I hope to help answer this question in the following chapters, by expanding on each of the eight emotional needs through the research and my own lived experience. Most importantly, I will provide plenty of guidance, encouragement and practical ideas for how to get your needs met where they are unfulfilled. Exploring the emotional needs in this sequential way will help you build the capacity and capabilities for deep and impactful solutions in your own life at home.

Truth be told, we've been stuffed full with the commercialization of home for so long – from unelected tastemakers telling us what the colour of the year is to seasonal promotions for kitchens or bedrooms or mudrooms we believe we need to install at once to stay 'on-trend'. I think it's time for a reset. I want to get back to basics and propose solutions that might use our hands but always come from the heart. Doing it this way means you'll be able to find ideas and opportunities within yourself, no matter where you live or what practical challenges exist in your home today. This all goes to say that there are plenty of gorgeous and well-written books which will help you find the right feng shui for your studio apartment or colourway for your dream hallway when that's what you need. I have those kinds of books, too, but this book isn't one of them. This book is about building and maintaining an *emotional connection* with your home so that you can live vibrantly there and beyond.

As the psychotherapist Esther Perel says, 'The quality of our relationships determines the quality of our lives.' Nowhere is this more apparent than the relationship we have with home.

1

Comfort

'There is nothing like staying at home, for real comfort.'

Jane Austen, *Emma*

WHEN I STARTED WRITING ABOUT home, I often took a Google Street View tour of the neighbourhoods I used to live in, which is how, one evening, I found myself outside the pixelated front door of my most formative childhood home. It was a tiny, terraced house in southern England that had all the classic proportions of a toddler's drawing. One door, two windows and a roof. The ground floor was three metres wide from wall to wall, roughly the same as a generous-size sofa. In fact, you could stay sitting on ours while shaking hands with visitors at the front door. Staring at the grainy rowhouse served up on my laptop, I was hit with a soupy mix of emotions. My husband peered over my shoulder as I explained that this used to be my home, and he said the same thing almost everyone had said or insinuated at the time: 'Gosh, it's small, isn't it?' It was an offhand comment, no more than the facts of the matter in front of him. But I felt the pulse of an old and familiar feeling lodged inside of me.

Growing up through the Bigger Is Better culture of the 1980s, I was conditioned to believe that a small home was something to be pitied because it was a symptom of failure. The cues were everywhere, from daytime soaps to blockbuster movies. Even when these well-to-do fictional families were miserable due to some heavily contrived drama, at least they all had their own bedrooms and en-suite bathrooms to go and cry in. I had many wild fantasies as a kid – most of which were conjured up daydreaming at my attic-bedroom window, which overlooked the car repair garage next door – but the one that recurred time and time again was to live in a home that looked like the ones I saw on TV.

Social conditioning casts a long shadow. The memories of my childhood home made me feel uncomfortable, like they were pushing against a bruise. I know from my work that feeling comfortable at home is so much more than lighting a few scented candles and sitting under a cashmere throw. It's about all the senses participating in an experience which provides complete ease. But reflecting on what was making me feel uncomfortable that evening suddenly made me think very differently about this core emotional need.

When I ask people what their home feels like, they most frequently talk about it feeling comfortable. It's an easy reach of a word, the first they come to because it sounds homely, I suspect. It's why comfort is the emotional need that regularly ranks the highest in terms of importance, globally, compared with the other seven. And yet there's a stubborn gap between what we say we want and how we actually feel. According to the most recent research, 27 per cent of people who say that comfort is important to have at home also say that they seldom get it where they live – this distance between their stated need and their lived reality is what the emotional gap represents. Why is comfort so hard to come by for as many as one in four people who want it? To find the answer, you have to move the throws and candles out of the way. I'm sorry, but these have become a distraction, touted through interiors trends that are heavily promoted through various social media platforms as a cosy silver bullet. We're all in thrall to these intoxicating solutions because they make it look so easy: *I can watch a reel, order some 'comfort' on Amazon and I'll get it the next day!*

One of the most enduring impacts of the social media content we consume all day is how much of people's interior lives we get to see, by which I mean their home interiors – living rooms, kitchens, bedrooms, and so on. Either as backdrop or in focus, we're exposed to so much domestic content that our frame of reference has expanded beyond our ability to contain it all. Where does that information go? A lot of it becomes a point of comparison. It's unsurprising that as many as 48 per cent of people say they don't feel their life at home is regularly reflected in the media. That's a lot of people, like you and me, scrolling on our phones, watching TV, streaming movies and receiving countless images of homes which bear little to no relation to our own. No one is immune to comparison. We've always wanted to keep up with the Joneses, the Jensens or the Jins, only now the people we're trying to level up with don't live next door but countless miles and income brackets away from us.

In this new reality, the persistent suggestions for cosy textiles and smells to dial up your comfort at home are about as effective as a bandage for a headache. There's a time and a place for plush cushions – and, yes, I love them too – but you have to get to the root of the feeling first. This is why comfort in IKEA's *Life at Home* research is defined as feeling content and at ease. And it's why starting from its opposite – *discomfort* – is the most helpful way into this complex emotion.

From all the conversations I've been privy to, I know there are various sources of discomfort with our living situations, but three recur the most:

- When we believe we have a limited amount of **space**
- When we believe we have too much **stuff**, which is badly organized
- When we're unhappy with the general **maintenance** and **cleanliness** of our home

Do you recognize your own pain-points in this list? I do. These forms of discomfort are most sharply felt when other people visit, and tend to be signalled by a completely unnecessary apology. You know the kind, because you've almost certainly made one yourself:

the apology for the clutter you didn't tidy up; the apology for not having enough space for people to put their bags, coats or shoes; the apology for the dodgy flush-function on the toilet or the old, noisy fridge or the stained armchair. Let's be clear: these are apologies for simply living in your own home.

It all confirms that our relationship with the practical aspects of our home is emotional, not functional. And the obsession with hacks for small-space living – something increasing numbers of us will be doing as populations grow and living quarters shrink – tends to be a lightning conductor neatly diverting attention away from ever grappling with our more complex feelings. Taking the time to sit with this revelation opened me up to a deeper well of emotions about my childhood home, and it was here that I found the work of Brené Brown to be of profound value.

Brown has been at the forefront of social research into shame, vulnerability and empathy for two decades, and it's her work on shame in particular that I find illuminating. Brown defines shame as 'the intensely painful feeling or experience of believing that we are flawed and therefore unworthy of love, belonging, and connection'. Was shame driving some of the reactions I witnessed when I walked through the front door of someone's home, whether it was a friend's or a research participant's? At first glance, it might feel like overreach to describe our compulsion to apologize for not clearing the table before guests come over as evidence of *shame*. But when I look at Brown's research, I see deep connections between shame and the emotional needs that underpin our feeling of home. Whilst we might not feel actively ashamed about our current living situation, or ever use the word to describe our experience, many of our behaviours and attitudes extend from residual feelings carried through from homemaking over the years. It might show up in otherwise quite unremarkable activities, like compulsively organizing things into boxes or keeping surfaces fastidiously clean. This means those recurring pain-points of 'space' and 'stuff' and 'cleanliness' aren't neutral concepts which you can just dress up with interior design solutions, then move on. You have to start by dealing with the deep and complex feelings people might have about their living situation.

By making this powerful connection between the practical aspects of home and our feelings about them, we can choose from a much bigger pool of solutions that reflect the functional *and* emotional tools at our disposal. No matter the size of the challenge, it's important to blend actions which are easy and quick to implement along with those that require more time for reflection. I call this my 'hands and heart' approach, and I'll use it throughout this book because I believe it can change your life at home right now and over the long term. But first, I want to tell you a story.

I was five years old when we moved into our two-up, two-down terraced house. I can't remember the moving day or what kind of work we did on it. The house emerges in my mind almost fully formed, although I know my parents likely exhausted themselves pouring their creativity into every available surface, turning the place into a home. Gig-fit from their art-student and squatting days, they were adept skip-scavengers. Huge planks of cast-off wood were frequently hauled through the front door to become bookshelves that ran the near-length of the property. My father painted a glorious sunrise-and-lark motif across my bedroom wall in the repurposed attic, followed by a series of countryside vignettes across the panels that blocked out my room from the eaves of the old roof, with leaping hares and gambolling lambs. The galley bathroom was proportional to – and therefore ideal for – an Ancient Egyptian tomb, which was vividly brought to life thanks to the life-size murals my father painted of Horus and Anubis overlooking the sarcophagus-themed tub. My parents even made Canopic jars out of papier mâché to hold our Body Shop bath pearls and soaps. I realize this makes it sound like we lived in a graduate art installation, but I can assure you that love and life plastered every wall. The effect was that it felt unmistakably like home. There was colour and clutter, laughter and tears, calm and chaos, food and music, living and dreaming. Somehow, too, there was room for it all in this tiny house. Our comfort cocoon.

But I couldn't stop the insidious creep of comparison – with the homes I saw in my favourite sitcoms and movies, with the homes of my friends. No one, real or imagined, seemed to live in a home like mine. Playdates at friends' houses often introduced me to the concept of entirely separate rooms dedicated to play, and to the 'breakfast bar'. At some point I crossed an invisible line between seeing the difference and *feeling* it. I don't know when the word 'small' started to curdle within me, but I can't remember a time when I didn't actively think about the size of our home and what I believed it said about me. I was aware of the acute financial strain my parents were under, thanks to their hushed conversations about money when they thought I was tucked up in bed. At school, where the mercy of a uniform irons out the most egregious differences between pupils, I could fudge the truth about where I lived and where we spent our summer holiday. The charade was harder to maintain if friends came back home with me, which meant I was very selective about inviting people over. And then I met Hayley.

Hayley looked like she was from central casting for happy-go-lucky teenage schoolgirls. Glossy hair swept into a ponytail, sun-kissed skin, cute tops, and so on. Just a few weeks into us knowing each other, she breezily suggested she walk home past my house so she could see where I lived. I instinctively knew that this new friend shouldn't – couldn't – see my home, that even explaining my home to someone like Hayley was beyond my ken. But it was like trying to stop a cannonball with my hands. Once she'd got the idea in her head, there was nothing I could do to prevent it. By the time we rounded the corner of my road, I was so frazzled with panic about how this encounter would play out that I was stumbling out in front of passing cars. Finally, we arrived at my front door, and I raced through a variety of insane lies to try out – *'This isn't my real home'*; *'These aren't my real parents'*; *'We're international spies and this is our cover'*. As my father greeted us, I saw her eyes flitting from the sofa to the kitchen, where cut-price cauliflower curry boiled on the hob. And then, 'Ohhh . . .' – that tilt of the head that indicated confusion, pity and something else, something more insidious. Disgust? The question left hanging in the air: *'Is that all there is?'* I squirmed, hoping for some merciful intervention like a bolt of lightning or collective amnesia. The miserable discomfort of it all took root deep inside me. Shame would stay with me for the next three decades.

Brené Brown's research into shame reveals that it almost overwhelmingly begins in childhood. An offhand comment from a parent, friend, sibling or teacher creates a split between who we are and how we think we are perceived. So much of shame centres on our social status, our relationships, and our health and well-being. It manifests in self-accusatory statements like 'I am not thin enough / rich enough / loving enough / good enough'. I was struck by what appears to be the domestication of shame, in that a lot of its branches extend from the spaces and places where we have lived. How many of us have found ourselves thinking 'My home is not big enough / clean enough / beautiful enough / good enough'? I'm aware it's not easy to claim shame. It's a tough word to hold in your mouth, making us feel guilty by association, as if we've done something wrong. Yet as Brown writes in *The Gifts of Imperfection*, 'We're all afraid of shame. The less we talk about shame, the more control it has over our lives.'

I want all of us to feel comfortable at home, which means we need to talk about shame. In doing so, we can claim back something that many of us have lost along the way: our authenticity. As Brown teaches through her work, those who demonstrate high levels of what she calls 'shame resilience' are living as authentically as possible. I love that Brown describes authenticity as 'a collection of choices that we have to make every day. It's about the choice to show up and be real. The choice to be honest. The choice to let our true selves be seen.' For a long time, I lost my authenticity at home to shame – until I made a choice not to. In order to feel full-bodied comfort at home, we all need to start making better choices about why and when we show up – and to stop making unnecessary apologies for where and how we live.

This is such important and grounding work, but it's tough to know where to begin. So, I want to suggest three demonstrable 'hands and heart' approaches that can help us all:

- Step away from unreasonable social expectations about your home
- Practise gratitude within the limits of your living situation
- Find and share your unique story about your own life at home

I'm not going to sugar-coat this: it's not easy work. But it builds a necessary foundation of comfort for life at home through which all our other emotional needs can flourish. So, let's begin.

Not-so-great expectations

Living in Denmark, I am frequently reminded that I've chosen one of the 'happiest nations in the world' to call home. The Nordic countries like to jostle for the top spot each year, but the consensus is that they've each got it all figured out somehow. Leaving aside the complexities of how you determine who is actually happy – and at what cost – the point I usually make in response to this claim is one the Danes themselves are quick to give: it's not about being happy, it's about being *content*. Semantics? Maybe, but one of the main reasons that the Danes are so content is because the gap between what they expect from life and what they have is very narrow. It's easier to feel content if you get what you expect, and the Danes simply place expectation where they can grasp it – like a six or a seven out of ten. You might wonder if this makes them dreamless bores, but all the innovation and culture exported from these shores over the years would suggest otherwise. I think this grip on reality makes them more grounded and able to free themselves from many of the unreasonable social expectations the rest of us place on ourselves, which we spend a lifetime trying, and usually failing, to reach.

It strikes me that this cultural phenomenon draws a very helpful parallel in our search for comfort. It shows us how we might all benefit from a more proportional view of where we sit in terms of our expectations for, and our reality of, home – especially with regard to how content we might feel there. From this perspective, we might be better equipped to define which – or, more pertinently, whose – norms we are reaching for, and how those norms serve us. It's tough-going, however. As Brown argues, 'We feel exhausted because without even giving it too much thought, most of us know that choosing authenticity in a culture that dictates everything from how much we're supposed to weigh to what our houses are supposed to look like is a huge undertaking.'

Choosing authenticity is harder than ever in the age of social media. We can apply filters that iron out our imperfections and create heavily edited versions of our lives that simply don't exist in the real world. When we stare through the looking-glass of our screens, we're in a version of life that's as unreal as Alice's Wonderland. Yet we use what we see there as evidence that we have fallen short. There may be some goodness in this artificial landscape, but research increasingly shows that social media use is linked to poor mental health, particularly amongst young people, with apps designed and marketed to appeal to Gen Z aesthetics.

Whenever we've explored the topic of technology in the home for the *Life at Home* Report, we've typically seen a fair split between those who see the positives and those who see the negatives, although it's worth remembering that technology takes on many shapes in our domestic lives, ranging from a virtual assistant like Alexa to vacuum cleaners. When it comes to social media, we know that some people (mostly skewing younger) feel more at home in online spaces and communities than where they live IRL. We also know that people of various ages and life-stages increasingly view the ideal home as a place to make money, which likely involves content creation featuring their interiors. You don't have to spend long on any of the Meta apps to see that many people have been extremely successful in promoting certain aesthetics and behaviours in the home, whether that's thrifty DIY or the rise of the palpably more insidious #TradWife trend.

Let's be clear: nearly all of this breezy content is impossible to recreate in your own home. I cannot tell you how many hours of my life I have lost watching reels of women in a full face of make-up cultivating their own yoghurt for a family of twelve, as if I, too, am going to wake before sunrise and strain unpasteurized milk curds into the earthenware pot I fired in my own kiln the previous weekend. Putting aside the insanity of squandering so much time staring at a never-ending series of social media posts whilst real life rages around me, the point is how this content makes me *feel*. Because it makes me feel kinda crappy – and I suspect I'm not alone in feeling this way. Every day, we stare through the looking-glass and compare our perfectly ordinary lives at home to an array of impossible scenarios on the other side. To take Brené Brown's line a step further, choosing authenticity *in a world of make-believe* is an even bigger undertaking. No wonder we're all exhausted.

The first, and most obvious, solution is to turn off

the (t)apps. Stop the social media feeds entirely, or at least brutally curate them. I know – *I know* – this feels like an impossible ask, so let me make it easier for you:

> → **Pick a wet Wednesday evening when you have nothing better to do, pull up your primary social media feeds and cull who you follow**
>
> Ask yourself: Does this person or that account make me feel good, bad or indifferent? When I did this exercise, I realized I was following hundreds – literally hundreds – of people whose content made me groan, roll my eyes, or feel a bit sad about my own life. And I was willingly letting this negative energy into my life. Every. Single. Day. Did you know that you don't have to follow anyone who makes you feel this way? Some of these people might know who you are, but the overwhelming majority don't know you exist. You are a minnow in a sea of followers. They will never know how you feel unless you tell them – but honestly, why bother? It's not about being right or wrong. Some self-appointed influencer has every right to be delighted with their bespoke new kitchen countertops and luxury holiday – and I don't need to have an opinion about it at all.

> **→ Be intentional about the kind of lifestyle and interiors inspiration you consume – and be sure to keep it time-limited and specific**
>
> Many of us fall into the same trap: we pin, save and bookmark interior design content that catches our eye, and then the algorithm continually pours similar bilge into our feed. We've become general enthusiasts for kitchen and bathroom renovation content, mesmerized by those three-year projects boiled down to a ninety-second reel, without anywhere to direct our energy if a kitchen or bathroom renovation isn't specifically and immediately happening in our own home. This mental lag only makes the distance between where you are and where you want to be feel even larger, and adds fuel to the frustration. My proposal? Use this content to inform your approach, help you learn new things and get inspired, but when your project is completed, it's best to mute these accounts or delete the app entirely.

I've worked through these approaches over the last few years, and I can attest to the liquid relief you'll feel when you release yourself from these unrealistic and disproportional expectations. Quite simply, you can't beat yourself up about something you can't see.

I'll be honest: I frequently stumble and find myself doomscrolling through countless photos, reels and videos of people I don't know, who live in homes that look nothing like mine, whilst the most tangible project I have on the horizon is cleaning the inside of my fridge. Comparison requires us to be constantly alert. I try to go easy on myself, knowing that social media is built on the back of the same functionality as online gambling, and our use of all these shiny, dopamine-boosting apps is increasingly described as an addiction. Of course, it's not just social media. We're all confronted with points of comparison in TV shows and films, in adverts and promotions, and by the simple matter of visiting friends and family who have homes and things and lives we want.

When the urge to gawk at other people's lives proves impossible to resist or I get hung up on what I feel I lack, I've started asking myself one simple but powerful question: *If I really want to live in that person's home, would I also be prepared to take on their life, knowing what little I do about it?* Would I still want an attic extension or an all-inclusive trip to the Maldives if it meant doing a job I hate, or regularly missing dinner with my kids, to pay for it all?

The answer, which is always no, helps me contextualize comparison so I can make it proportional to my own life at home. Reducing the overall input, especially on social media, definitely makes it easier to handle. But making a *conscious choice* about what to do with comparison is where the solution truly lies. Remember that we don't get to see the whole picture of someone else's life at home, even those of our friends and family. It's just a filtered snapshot. Remember, too, that most things which look deceptively easy are hard to obtain, and nothing comes without a cost – financial, emotional or otherwise.

To go back to the example set by the Danes, when we hold ourselves accountable to the things we think we want in our own lives at home, we find ourselves far closer to both expectation and reality – and much more content.

The limit does not exist

When I was twelve, my parents took me and my sister to Ireland for a summer holiday. We spent the first few weeks in a tiny seaside town in Northern Ireland, staying in an old fisherman's cottage which had two rooms, no running water and a chemical toilet in the garden. It was glorified camping. We had to walk up a hill to fetch water from a well, and wash ourselves with a cup whilst standing in a plastic bowl. It wasn't the kind of summer holiday my school friends were having, that's for sure. Yet my abiding memories are warm and happy.

By the time we were nice and ripe from all the pat-down showers, we drove to Dublin where my parents had arranged a two-week house exchange with old friends. We'd never been to this house before, and given this was life before high-speed internet and Google-anything, we had no visuals to go on, just an address and an Ordnance Survey map. In our mind's eye, this leg of the holiday promised to be the salve to our summer hardship. We pictured leisurely baths and comfy beds with fresh linen. I was mildly mortified that this poor family would have to stay in our tiny terraced house, back in England.

On arrival, it became abundantly clear that you could fit this house into ours twice over, and still have room to spare. This was a single-storey, white-washed rowhouse, with two separate bedrooms somehow carved out for the children, whilst the parents slept on a sofa-bed in the front room. I was given the single room at the back, and my sister slept in what appeared to be a converted larder, replete with cans of tuna and chopped tomatoes under the bed. When my parents pulled out their mattress for the night, it ran from wall to wall – meaning the fridge, oven, and any cupboards and drawers couldn't be opened until it was folded away again. Suffice to say that my fantasies of lounging around a stately Dublin townhouse had been dashed on the cobbles outside, the moment we pulled up. I suddenly ached for home.

Looking back, I'm not sure how my parents lasted a month on the road with two young kids and accommodation that seemed to mock the very idea of comfort, without losing their minds. But I can tell you this: when we finally got home, it was like someone had swapped out my regular eyeballs for widescreen versions. Our little house welcomed us with big, open arms, providing plenty of room to rest, eat together, and pack away our cherished things. 'Look,' my mother cooed from the front room, 'I can stretch my legs without accidentally turning on the TV!'

This experience taught me the single most valuable lesson about creating a better life at home: **absolutely nothing has to change in your home for you to feel like it's a completely different place**. With the benefit of hindsight, I understand that what I was experiencing was gratitude. I'd become so accustomed to pointing out what my home lacked, I'd stopped noticing everything it had. This childhood home is where I learned the power of my imagination and how to conjure up big ideas for myself. It's where I learned about love and resilience and hope. And I was grateful for it all.

Being told to be grateful can feel like a rebuke, as if we're petulant children being told off for expecting something different or better. Gratitude isn't about scolding; it's about appreciation for what you have, even when you wish for more. I believe that gratitude is an activity, too, best executed through regular practice by observing the things in your life that make you feel good. The great thing about gratitude is that there's no limit to how much you can feel, and no rules for what can prompt it. There's no better place to practise gratitude than where you live, either. You can be grateful for literally anything in your home, from a particular coat hook to that time your best friend stayed over to wipe away your tears after a bad break-up.

If you're already in the habit of practising gratitude, whether that's with tools like a gratitude journal or through prayer and reflection, then it might feel natural to shift your focus to your home. But if gratitude is something you've not intentionally deployed recently, I have a lovely exercise that can help you on your way.

I want you to walk slowly around your home and to look at everything around you with open eyes and ears:

> → Find one **object**, one **area** and one **activity** in your home that makes you feel good.
>
> Use your senses to help you navigate, remembering the importance of smell and touch in addition to what you can see. These three things might all be in the same space, or they might be scattered around. Note them down – these are your **'gratitude anchors'**.
>
> If you don't feel too self-conscious doing so, say a little thank-you out loud to these things. It helps move the gratitude from your head to your heart.

Now, you can use your gratitude anchors in two ways:

> → When the spectre of comparison looms, and you worry and rage that you lack the things you want, reach for your gratitude anchors to bring you back home. **Go and hold that object, stand in that space, or do that activity.** Your home already holds so much comfort for you.

> **Ask yourself what it is you love about your gratitude anchors, and use those insights to inform other parts of your life at home that feel challenging.** By targeting certain 'hot spots' with the knowledge and wherewithal you already enjoy and practise at home, you can create more comfort in a way that's authentic, manageable and longer-lasting.

I'll tell you my own three things:

My object: a coffee mug. It's one of those American diner mugs; it has the perfect weight and a chunky rim, and I love how it feels to drink from it, particularly if I have a cup of tea in bed. My husband took it from an illegal flatshare when he was living in New York, years before he met me, and it reminds me of the fact that this mug has been through multiple house-moves across countries and lived to tell the tale, just like me. I always reach for that mug first, if I have my pick on any given day. Then I know that the next twenty-odd minutes, whilst I sip my tea, will be good.

My area: my children's bedroom. It used to be our spare-room-slash-study, and when I was first pregnant and contemplating bringing a baby into our tiny apartment, I raged at the injustice of losing my room for writing in so we could have a nursery instead. Now it's one of my favourite places to be. Sometimes I just stand there in the middle of the day, if my husband is out with the kids and I'm home alone, and gaze at all the mad and wonderful things that my children collect around them: all the favourite teddies; the kindergarten paintings tacked to the wall; my daughter's weird little pebble and curio collection; the beaded bracelets with our names on. I might have lost a room, but I gained a world.

My activity: watching movies on the sofa with my family. Now my daughter is old enough for a full movie viewing, she insists on popcorn and hot chocolate with marshmallows whilst rewatching some Disney film for the billionth time. She likes to pull an old blanket over her knees, like a little old lady, and she'll shuffle over for a cuddle during the scary scenes. Most of the time, I've got a thousand other things to be getting on with instead, from replying to emails to folding laundry, but I know these moments are finite. One day my daughter will be too big to snuggle in my arms, she won't need reassurance during the frightening bits, and her parents will be too old and tragic to watch Disney movies with. So, I give thanks for each time she asks to watch 'a moobie' and gladly go and whip up the hot chocolate before taking my designated spot on the sofa.

Practising gratitude is like exercising a muscle. You have to do it regularly to keep it in shape. Focusing on a handful of gratitude anchors helps you maintain a regular habit that will soon become second nature. Before you know it, you'll be finding reasons to be comfortable where you live without having to think about it – and without having to change a thing.

Tell your story

Just before Christmas 2019, during one of our IKEA research events in a townhouse in South London, I met a blogger and young mother who had flown over to join us from New York. I was pregnant with my daughter, and Ellen happened to be expecting her third child around the same time, so we got to chatting and swapping stories.

I soon discovered that Ellen lived in a 45-square-metre, one-bedroom apartment in the attic of a brownstone building in Brooklyn with her partner and two young kids. She loved the period features and lived-in warmth of her home, and the lively neighbourhood that spilled out around the stoop, where they frequently chatted to passers-by and ate ice cream when the weather was warm. She was less enamoured with the lack of space, but they made it work because life at home for Ellen was constantly growing, even if their floor plan wasn't. She showed me a delicate drawing she had made of the layout, marking where the windows, beds and tables were. I felt my breath catch. It was hard not to wonder at the prospect of her bringing another child into the mix, or to clumsily ask where the crib would go or where she would do her work. It was hard not to imply, with that imperceptible pity-tilt of my head, *wouldn't a bigger home be better for your family*?

And suddenly there it was again, the tendrils coiling out from the shame pitted deep inside me. I started reckoning with my own unresolved feelings, close to asking her – no, expecting her – to explain why she wasn't preoccupied with doing it the 'proper' way like so many others were. That unspoken assumption was racing through my mind: *'Couldn't you get more space if you just, you know, tried a bit harder?'*

I went to bed that night weighed down by my feelings. My reaction to Ellen's situation wasn't about her; it was about me. It was about the fact that my husband and I were going to have our first child and I was still holding fast to the lie that 'real families' lived in large suburban houses with playrooms and guestrooms and gardens – because that's what decades of social conditioning and unrealistic media portrayals had shown me. By comparison, we lived up four flights of stairs in a small apartment in the city centre, with a shared courtyard and rats in the basement. I was ashamed I hadn't done better for myself. And I was preemptively ashamed of how my child would feel about the size and capabilities of our home, and how they would explain it to their friends who eventually came to visit. My shame ran so deep, I was at risk of making it intergenerational.

When I met Ellen, one of the things that surprised me most was that she talked about her tiny home with such kindness and ease. This was evident through her blog, too, where she had built an identity and a community around small-space living. She even admitted to her readers that there was a certain vulnerability in sharing something that should be as matter-of-fact as a small-space floorplan. It's one thing to tell people you live in a small home; it's quite another to lay your cards on the table and let people do the maths for themselves. But Ellen was driving the narrative about her home rather than letting shame do the talking. She was creating connections around a subject that might otherwise feel isolating. She held up her life at home for all to see, and did not find it lacking.

This was pivotal for me. For all the ways in which I had reset my expectations about my life at home, I had failed to tell this part of my story. Another irony not lost on me was that, as a writer, I had written my way through a lot of challenging topics but had never once managed to commit words to a page on this particular matter, of shame. As Brené Brown asserts, shame and its clutch of associated feelings 'thrive on silence'. The best thing we can do is speak shame into submission.

I'm not suggesting that we all need to start chronicling our true domestic lives on TikTok or Instagram, or write books about it (hello!). But there are two easy and accessible actions you can take to start framing your own narrative about your unique life at home:

> → **Talk to your friends and family.** I want you to find your go-to person who creates a safe space for you to name your domestic discomfort, then open up to them and encourage them to do the same. There

are lots of things I talk to my husband about, but I have a gaggle of close friends who have helped me share my feelings about all the anxieties and frustrations I face at home because they have relatable experiences in their home lives too. I always feel lighter and brighter after I've put down the load to see I'm not the only one carrying something like it.

→ **Write a letter to your home.** It might be the one you live in now, or a formative one from your past. Tell it how you really feel – give it both barrels if you need to. You might put pen to paper, record a voice note, or lie down and let your thoughts flow. No matter the format, just get the words out of you. Be honest and unfiltered – your home is never going to read it! I've done this exercise a few times (including letters to people I will *never, ever* send), and it feels like sharing a secret that's been curdling inside me. The relief is palpable.

When I talk and write about my honest experiences of homemaking, I find a community of people who want to share their experiences with me, too. Most of what I have to say, despite it feeling so singular to my life, is deeply relatable to others, who often chime in with a chorus of 'Gah, tell me about it . . .' and 'Me too!' It's that James Joyce line: 'In the particular is contained the universal.' I encourage you to tell your story, so we might grow that community together.

Inspired by the internet-enabled tour of my childhood neighbourhood when I began writing this chapter, I started digging around for any other information I could find about that old address. I came across a relatively recent estate-agent listing, but its strangely staged photographs of my old home bore no likeness to the place I remembered. Every single room was painted white, with characterless new bathroom and kitchen units, and laminate covering the gorgeously knotted and historic oak floorboards. Gone, too, were the murals – the rising skylark and the gambolling lambs, the Egyptian gods ushering us into the afterlife with their gifts, the *fleur de lys* above our dining table – all erased with a tub of cheap emulsion. My old home was a ghost of itself. There was no colour, and no life. I felt winded.

Then I noticed the floorplan. The cards were laid out on the table, begging me to do the maths. The square footage was identical to the home I live in today, almost to the centimetre. The coincidence stunned me as I sat back in my chair, staring at the black lines that suddenly represented both the footprint of my childhood and an imprint of my life today. I thought of the colour and the clutter, and the laughter and the tears, the calm and the chaos, all those years ago. I thought about the fact that there is as much room for it all in my tiny home today – my comfort cocoon. I held up my life at home and, finally, I did not find it lacking.

I'll be honest: I didn't anticipate writing about shame when I set out my thoughts on the feeling of comfort. I thought I'd come at it from the familiar framing of our senses, writing about the importance of the whole-body experience of a comfortable home, from sight to smell. Certainly, this sensory aspect is an important dimension of homemaking. But the more I looked back at the research, the comments that people made during my home visits for IKEA, and the rich memories of my own experiences, the better I could see that comfort is layered like an onion. On the surface we see cosy throws and scented candles, but at its heart comfort is about **living authentically** and **without constraint** in our own home. If we don't deal with what makes us feel uncomfortable where we live, our homes will be rotten at the core.

As you reflect on the insights and solutions covered in this chapter, and the powerful connection between our functional home and the deep feelings we have about living there, please extend some tenderness to yourself. When we dig into a rich seam of emotion, we frequently set off small tremors which unearth old (and sometimes difficult) memories. We might also come face to face with aspects of our life at home today that we hadn't questioned before. If this is the case, just remember that building a great relationship with your home means you get to honour all the experiences of homemaking in your life, even the tough ones. Allow yourself to sit with all the feelings and memories, knowing they will be of extraordinary service to you when you're ready.

2

Control

'The most common way people give up their power is by thinking they don't have any.'

Alice Walker

IN THERAPY, THERE'S A CLASSIC question – more an adage, really – that goes something like this: 'Do you want to be right, or do you want to be happy?' I first came across it in the work of Esther Perel, the popular psychotherapist and relationship therapist. She writes about asking a young couple in her office if they would each rather be right or be married. It's more a provocation than a question, an opportunity to reflect on whether it's possible to sustain a relationship on absolutes alone. Elaborating on the acute tension that occupied the room, she writes: 'When we heighten the discomfort we feel around how stuck we are, we urgently start to reconnect with our sense of agency.' Reading this, it felt like a door suddenly opened up between two of the foundational emotional needs of the home – comfort and control.

This got me thinking in a deeper way about the language of relationships and the parallels between our love life and our home life. Certainly, in almost every relationship there are disagreements and arguments. Most therapists will tell you that the kind of fights couples tend to have can be boiled down to a handful of recurring themes. One of these fights, according to Perel, is about control and power. This kind of fight might be expressed through arguments about who has the say over household finances, for example, or how a couple spends their time together and apart. When I look at all the emotional needs connected to homemaking, I have to wonder if our need to feel in control – and what happens if we don't – is a trigger for a recurring fight we have with our own home. When we talk about feeling in control of our life at home, are we actually talking about having and maintaining power?

When I reflect on the times in my homemaking life when I've felt the most powerless, they neatly align with the times I've lived in rental accommodation. Of the twenty-five-plus places I've called home, the overwhelming majority have been rented. Renting from an administration, a remote agent or a live-in landlord, it's all versions of the same message: hand over the cash as you're passing through. No wonder Monopoly was originally called The Landlord's Game.

My experience of renting is consistent with the rise

of a particularly insidious form of rental arrangement – that between a tenant and an unregulated private landlord. This is a situation the UK, in particular, has seen almost double in the last twenty years as the price of housing has outpaced the rise in incomes by some measure. In Denmark, a study from 2020 looking at the same issue concluded that 'when finding reasonably priced accommodation is next to impossible' (as is the case in the capital, Copenhagen), the economic growth of cities is severely hampered by a less mobile workforce. This is one way to look at the problem – as a cost-centre issue. The other is to address the debilitating mental and physical health impact of unaffordable and unavailable housing on people who have run out of options. At the sharper end, countless people are staring into the abyss of temporary housing for weeks, months, even years. These are people living with extended family members whose patience is wearing thin; crashing on a friend's sofa for a few nights until they've overstayed their welcome; spending one or two weeks in an Airbnb at grotesquely inflated prices just to bridge the gap. You might have experienced these situations yourself. If so, you'll know that temporary housing is not a home. It's why millions of people who technically have a roof over their head are still considered homeless. Not being in control of where and how you live renders you powerless.

I hadn't accounted for how badly the psychic grip of living month-to-month in a rented property, with a large deposit locked up in a distant landlord's bank account, had affected me until I was thirty-four and held the keys to my own home for the first time. Although homeownership is how the majority of people live in the EU (70 per cent own their home, according to 2021 figures from Eurostat), the proportion differs significantly across member states. Denmark sits in the bottom three, just above Germany where the split is almost exactly 50/50 between homeowners and tenants.

The idea of 'ownership' was something that came through very strongly when we first started mapping the emotional needs of the home through the IKEA *Life at Home* Report, back in 2018. In fact, if you go back and read that year's report, we list ownership as one of the first five emotional needs we had in scope at the time. But in the two or three years that followed, from the kinds of conversations we were having through home visits and exploring the deep impact of the pandemic, we heard that people experienced ownership in a variety of ways. It went far beyond the matter of getting a mortgage. What they wanted was a deep and meaningful sense of control over their domestic surroundings. This expansion in meaning hasn't done much to close the emotional gap, however. The most recent data show that of the people who say control is important at home, 28 per cent on average seldom experience it. The gap is inevitably larger amongst renters and younger people, and smaller amongst homeowners and older people.

In my case, I found that taking on a mortgage came with its own set of complex feelings, but it was like someone had given me a key to a secret door in my homemaking journey. It was the first time I felt fully in control of my living situation. No one was going to increase my rent or tell me to move out. No one was going to dictate what I could and couldn't do to the interior design, at the risk of losing a massive chunk of change. There was a hungry sort of power to it that I grabbed at, like someone had offered me food after a fast.

It meant that everything was going to feel easier now, right?

When I was thirteen, I moved with my family from our tiny terraced home to a four-bedroom house in a suburban estate in Middle England. There were no hand-painted murals or marionette puppets hanging from the walls. Now it was greige paint jobs and wall-to-wall carpets. In many ways, this new home soothed many of my shame-filled worries because it quite literally looked like every other house on the estate. So much so, in fact, the first time I took the bus back from the city centre on my own, I had a panic attack because I didn't know which place was ours.

Inside, it was immediately clear that none of the interiors were to my parents' taste. Not only was every floor covered in the kind of industrial fitted carpet you find in offices, but most of the rooms were wallpapered in a twee arrangement of canary yellow stripes and floral mock wainscoting. Ordinarily my parents would have spent five minutes in that place then ripped the lot out. But this was a rental. Now we were in thrall to the remote and almighty power of The Deposit, which seemed to be in a constantly perilous state of existence, capable of vanishing if we so much as spilled juice on the floor. This shift in power and control created a palpable sense of anxiety that lived alongside us, like a feckless flatmate, for the next two years.

We were not alone in our feelings. Around four in five people regularly feel frustrated with their home, most often citing too much clutter or the number of chores as the biggest problem. The rub is that people who rent are more likely to feel frustrated than those who own. Renters are also less likely to experience enjoyment at home, compared with homeowners. Forget having a place for everything and living authentically; simply throwing a party or using a cup without a coaster feels better when you feel in control of your environment – and you're more likely to feel in control if you own where you live. What's more, the ability to make changes to your home is closely connected to your mental health, to the extent that people who adapt their home environment are 40 per cent more likely to say their mental health improved during the time they made changes, compared with people who make no changes at all. And – surprise, surprise – changing your environment feels easier when you own, rather than rent. On and on and on it goes.

All of this begs the question: Do we need to own our home to feel in control of our surroundings? It's certainly true that renting might make it harder to change our surroundings, if the landlord makes the rules. But the *Life at Home* research reveals five consistent barriers that stop people from taking control and making changes to their own life at home – and they apply across a variety of different living situations, including both renting and homeownership:

- Lack of space
- Lack of time
- Lack of money
- Lack of permission
- Lack of practical know-how

I can tell you, from lived experience, that these challenges are by no means unique to renting and that simply owning your own home isn't going to fix the problem. On the surface, these barriers appear quite matter-of-fact because it's true that working parents are pretty time-strapped, for example, and people on the minimum wage lack additional funds for home improvement, and so on. If we look at the barriers in this way, we may find ourselves muttering that oft-repeated line: 'If only I had more time / money / space / ability' (choose your own pain-point), which might feel intractable but is also a neat way of absolving us of individual responsibility. Increasingly, the solutions lie in how we see ourselves in relation to the challenges in front of us. We have to *choose* to move beyond them, rather than waiting for things to change around us. As the iconic entertainer Carol Burnett said, 'Only I can change my life. No one can do it for me.' All too often, the stories we repeatedly tell ourselves about our inability to change our home environment simply become the truth. From the conversations I've been part of, it seems that many of us do as much as we can to maintain that reality for as long as possible, even when it clearly doesn't serve us. It's just easier to live with the status quo.

Unpacking these barriers helped me look at the feeling of control from a different angle. Control is less about power – over our home, over our circumstances – and far more about agency and choice. This is how we have come to define control in the *Life at Home* research. It's about having agency over our environment. When we feel in control, we're exercising our agency and are able to make choices that are good for us. Many of us lack control in our domestic lives because we coexist with a very real fear of the consequences our choices might leave us with. And, yes, this is exacerbated for those who rent, given that renters are limited by the ways we can personalize our home because our rental contract tells us so, and constrained by the financial fallout if we do. *Will this nail in the wall cost me hundreds of pounds? What's 'reasonable wear and tear'?* These were the questions that plagued my parents for all the time we lived in that cookie-cutter rental, to the point of distraction.

Beyond the presence of a landlord, there are many other reasons why we might experience a lack of control over our home, even if we own the deeds. There may be many differing needs and expectations amongst the people we live with, for example. Or we might not believe in our abilities or aesthetic judgement to make the changes we want. Holding the keys to my own home after decades of renting prompted a deep question: *What does control actually feel like, even when you're the one paying the mortgage?*

Just as I did in Chapter 1, I want to propose some 'hands and heart' solutions. These are organized around four ways to create a feeling of control, no matter your living situation:

- Bring the natural world into your home
- Pause for reflection
- Get curious
- Focus on the doing, not the having

We'll start with the quick and easy things you can do, and finish with some deeper approaches that you'll cherish in the long run.

Green fingers

Did you know that having and making choices is something we are hardwired to establish, pretty much from birth? There's a fascinating research paper from 2010, 'Born to choose', which reviews the scientific literature on control and concludes that 'belief in one's ability to exert control over the environment and to produce desired results is essential for an individual's well-being.' The authors present evidence that there's 'a biological basis for the need for control and for choice' and conclude that the need for both is 'imperative for survival'. This is why we shouldn't underestimate the impact of hanging a favourite picture or painting a wall a colour we love. In short, we don't want to be given choices and control because we're being difficult, but because we *cannot live without them*.

In life, the choices we make bolster our growth and identity. Good choices inform healthy growth; bad choices inform unhealthy growth. Take cooking – something my father has done daily for decades, with relish and joyful chaos, merrily throwing things into sauces and oils, and then into pans and on to plates, to feed his delighted family. The carpeted kitchen in our rental home must have been installed by someone who hadn't prepared or eaten a meal in their entire life. Suffice to say, my father's cooking style was at odds with his environment, and wore my mother's patience as thin as the carpeted floor she routinely spot-cleaned and cursed. But what was the alternative? Should my father have stopped cooking the meals we all loved to eat together? Clean floors or happy kids. I can only imagine how many of the interior design choices made by the landlord that came with the rental home my parents took on must have forced similarly exhausting decisions and consequences.

Choice, then – no matter how small – is imperative to our survival at home. It's the reason you feel like you're dying inside when you're really stuck and out of control. Knowing where or how to begin to remedy this can feel overwhelming, especially when your nervous system is shot to pieces if you're living under a deposit diktat. So, let's start with one simple, non-permanent solution. This solution can realign the balance of power and help you reassert your agency, and it has the additional benefit of having proven health benefits. You see, there are plenty of blogs, books and TV shows that provide fantastic advice on the kinds of temporary interior design solutions you can use on spaces that are constrained by challenges, from removable wallpaper to cushions and rugs you can take with you when you leave. These are all great approaches, in time. But if you're looking for something *really* easy to start with – something which is the very definition of healthy growth – you can't go wrong with greenery.

Plants, whether they're cut, potted, dried or fake, are my go-to for those moments when I feel overwhelmed by the scale of things I want to change in my life at home. The great thing about greenery is that it deftly cuts across the five main barriers to change and control:

- A simple pot plant takes up very little **space**
- You don't need much **time** at all to arrange a new bouquet in a vase
- You can grow your own from a **cheap** packet of seeds, or use the stones or seeds from fruit and veg you've eaten
- No one, not even an overbearing landlord, has to give you **permission** to bring a little greenery into your home

- Whilst watering a plant requires very little **practical know-how**, if you're convinced something living won't survive a week in your care, then dried or fake plants are solid alternatives

What's more, the benefits to having greenery indoors are manifold. Biophilia is the innate human connection we have with nature, and our proximity to plants and other living things has been extensively shown to make us feel happier and healthier in body and mind. Not only are natural colours and shapes lovely and calming to look at, but plants are handy air detoxifiers which help keep indoor spaces cleaner and more temperate. No wonder that the *Life at Home* research which straddled the years of the pandemic showed that people were more likely to say that access to greenery was important in an ideal home, and as many as one in ten people have spoken to their plants. Plant parenthood is having its moment in the sun.

Greenery also lets you take a tentative step into making other non-permanent design choices for your home through the kinds of pots and vases you put them in. I'll defer to interiors experts here for colourways and textures, but personally speaking I believe you can't go wrong with a classic terracotta pot for a plant and a clear glass vase for cut flowers. I learned that from my parents. For all the things that were strictly out in that place we called home for two years in the 1990s, plants were definitely in. In fact, there's a plant that lived with us in that rental home, with the wall-to-wall carpets, which continues to thrive in the house my parents went on to live in for the next two decades and counting. Life will always find a way.

Say a little prayer

I'm not religious. I don't practise a form of faith which points towards a God or gods, or that asks me to follow scripture or attend specific places of worship. But I'm up for a lot of stuff that people might categorize as 'spiritual'. I'll take an Angel Card at my weekly yoga class; I've got crystals charging under the full moon; and I'll gladly spend an evening in the company of a good mate and a pack of tarot cards. While I'm not one of *those* people – the ones who live and breathe some mystical creed and wear a lot of hemp – if there's even a small chance that some of these 'woo-woo' practices might work, sign me up. And I see it all the time, this split between the rational and the spiritual as we try to make sense of the world. Sometimes logic fails us. This is all to say that my second suggestion for readying ourselves for change and control might feel a little out of character, given that it's best known as the Serenity Prayer.

You've probably heard it, or at least some version of it: 'Grant me the serenity to accept the things I cannot change, the courage to change the things I can, and the wisdom to know the difference.' It's probably best known for being integrated into the Alcoholics Anonymous programme, which uses it as a grounding moment for those attending meetings. A prayer is essentially an earnest request for hope, and the ones that are oft-repeated, in rhythm and syntax we can easily remember, are requests for hopes we all share. And who doesn't want more patience, courage and wisdom? The point about this prayer, or mantra, is that it asks us to delineate the world into things we can control and things we can't, and to recognize on which side things have fallen.

This is what the Stoics were all about, of course. Stoicism is a school of philosophy that flourished in Ancient Greece and Rome which placed a high value on virtue as the path to a happy life. The consequence of this thinking made the Stoics emotionally resilient to things going wrong. If you're looking for some neat aphorisms about life, then the Stoics came out with some doozies. In fact, many of them read as ancient precursors to the Serenity Prayer, like this line from Epictetus: 'Make the best of what is in our power, and take the rest as it occurs.' There are two notable benefits to this kind of approach:

* **When we stop fixating on what we resolutely cannot change – usually the most frustrating and distracting things – it frees our mental energy to focus on things that *are* in our control**
  I don't have the time, money or skills to renovate my kitchen, and watching my neighbours and countless friends do just that makes me feel perpetually frustrated

and stuck. But I can (just about) put up new shelves, plant some herbs and splash out on a decent frying pan, so I'll direct my energy to things, instead, which are currently in my control.

* **It's a useful exercise in making us reflect on some of the stories we have repeatedly told ourselves about what is in our control** Esther Perel captures this notion perfectly: 'When I tell people to "write often and edit well", what I mean is this: we are not in control of how life unfolds, but we have agency over how we structure and interpret it. And those new interpretations can help us get unstuck and give us the freedom to make adult choices that we couldn't as children. New stories can liberate us from defeating narratives, predetermined thinking, and forgone conclusions. They create hope and possibilities for change.' Amen to that.

Understanding this split between what we can control, and what we cannot, is a great way of balancing structure and spontaneity in our lives. I've often struggled with situations where I cannot control the outcome. I get impatient when things don't happen according to the timeline in my mind. And I'm very results-driven, which means I find it hard to accept I've done a good job unless I can point to demonstrable success or someone pats me on the back. And then life happens, and all the best-laid plans go the way of the wind. If this rings true for you, then find solace in knowing that folding spontaneity into your domestic life on a foundation of structure makes it all the richer and more rewarding, and a lot more fun. The Serenity Prayer, along with the principles of Stoicism, is a way to establish this balance. It gives us a way of assessing and handling the things we cannot control so they provide new opportunities, rather than closed doors.

Ask a better question

It's happened to the best of us. You're at a dinner party or a work thing, and you're stuck next to someone who doesn't know how to have a conversation. Perhaps they don't ask a single question, leaving you to carry the burden, or they ask the boring kind that's practically dead on arrival, like 'What do you do for a living?' I'm guilty of asking those kinds of questions, too. But lately I've taken to striking out further afield. Asking better questions is how we have richer conversations, an exchange that offers us depth and insight into the people and places we encounter. So, what makes a *better* question, and how can we use this to help us navigate control in our life at home?

The stories we repeatedly tell ourselves about what we can and cannot do are often the consequence of not asking good enough questions – of ourselves, of the people around us, and of the situations we find ourselves in. There are many examples of this from the kinds of questions we ask during the interviews we conduct during IKEA research home visits. These interviews are designed to bring up information we don't otherwise have about how people live. If the motivation is to understand what kinds of things people do at home so we can design products that help them, then you might ask someone, 'Where do you eat dinner?' or 'Where do you store your shoes?' But if the motivation is to understand how people *feel* about their home, so we can help them feel better, then you might ask someone, 'What does an ideal dinner with your family or friends look like?' or 'Can you tell me how you feel in the morning when you're getting ready to leave your home?' When we're motivated to understand how people *feel*, and not just what they do, we create a connection that opens up richer and more rewarding opportunities for change. The good news is that it's easy to turn this point of reflection on yourself. Let me give you a prime example of this from my own life at home.

My apartment does not have a huge amount of storage space. I mean, it doesn't have much space, full stop. The front door opens into our narrow hallway and kitchen, so when people come over they tend to leave their shoes on the doormat outside and I throw their coats towards our overstuffed hooks and hope for the best. When our daughter comes home from kindergarten, she immediately wants to release her body from the clothing we've shackled her with, especially when it's winter, which in Denmark is essentially nine months of the year. Picture the scene: she's bedecked in a bike helmet, snowsuit, boots, hat, gloves, jumper . . . and it all comes off in the hallway, cast on to the floor for us to scoop up behind her and put, well . . . somewhere?

One typical morning, as two working parents with packed calendars, a commute, a baby and a toddler on the verge of a meltdown, our efforts to track down her missing glove after breakfast were close to shredding our last nerves. My immediate thought was that we needed a better storage system: designated spots for helmets, hats, gloves, shoes, and so on. I figured I just needed to wrestle control over the situation by implementing some functional hacks to our limited space and making sure everyone followed the rules.

That's because I asked myself the rather unimaginative question, *Where can I store my kid's stuff?* And because we live in a small apartment, the answer felt constrained by my lack of options. It means that I reached a solution which, on the face of it, mostly met my needs – a storage box in the hallway cupboard and a small shoe rack in her bedroom. But there were still many Big Feelings each morning. So, I became curious, and I asked: *What would a great morning look like?*

This more generous and empathetic question helped me spot the things that would make the difference to our morning routine, turning it from an adrenaline-laden nightmare to a loving nudge into the outside world. It helped me see that my daughter reacts badly when she senses we're time-constrained and stressed, so I started getting up half an hour earlier when I needed to do a long commute so I could be washed and dressed before she woke up. It helped me see that breakfast was often where my daughter cherished practising new skills, like spreading her own jam, so we needed to protect that time at the expense of other things we might want to get done before work. It also helped me see that the single most important part of my morning is telling my family I love them and kissing them goodbye. All too often those simple exchanges went missing when we were trying to find lost clothing or manhandling our screaming daughter into her jacket. Asking a better question got me to acknowledge what was important, and then I could make a wider range of changes that were in my control, which honoured it.

Asking better questions helps you move beyond the assumptions you've made about yourself and your circumstances. It lets you become an active participant in your home rather than a passive occupant. I'll give you a handful to help get you started:

- What makes you smile in the morning?
- When was the last time you cooked a meal you really enjoyed?
- What does it take to get a great night's sleep?

These are three simple, exploratory questions you can try answering today. Of course, there are also questions that elicit the standard refrain 'You won't know until you ask . . .', such as: *What if you asked your landlord for permission to paint your bedroom wall? What if you asked your friend to teach you how to put up a shelf?* And so on. The questions are endless, and so are the opportunities for you to make a change.

It's what you do that counts

My husband and I have a few talents between us, but none of them extend to DIY. When we first moved into our own home, where we live today, we had to invite friends over for coffee in order to get them to hang pictures for us.

So, faced with the opportunity to substantially alter the interior of our new home, we panicked, scraped together whatever pennies we had left, and paid a man with a ladder and a toolbelt to come and do the work. The changes were minimal, just repainting walls and sanding floors, because we could afford little else, but making those choices – the very specific green-blue colour of the living-room walls, the kind of lacquer on the floorboards – was enough for us to feel that we had taken control of our new surroundings and made them ours.

This is why I'm in awe of people who are fearless about DIY. The kind of people who buy literal wrecks and turn them into mid-century-modern places of wonder entirely on their own, self-taught from YouTube on the basics of plumbing to plastering. And then, when they're done, *they go and do it all over again somewhere else.* Returning to my principles in the previous chapter, I've had to stop watching these kinds of addictive social media accounts – the ones where people condense a three-year renovation project into ninety seconds – because the difference between us is too large to straddle and it makes me feel nauseous.

My point is that there is a lot I'd like to change about my home, but doing so would require an extensive amount of money or expertise, and I have neither right now. This brings me up short, sometimes, when I'm feeling exasperated about the state of things and wail at my family. If you also have moments when you're tired and sad and angry because you can't find the time, money, ability or permission to do what you want, remember what Maya Angelou said: 'I've learned that people will forget what you said, people will forget what you did, but people will never forget how you made them feel.' This is deeply applicable to home, where our fondest memories of the spaces and places where we have lived are almost always of the feelings we had during particular experiences there. When it comes to our interiors, activities trump aesthetics every time. So, here's an exercise to try:

> → **Think of three great experiences you've had at home** – either your own or someone else's – that you could recreate without needing to make any material changes or additions to your home.
>
> I'll start you off with an easy one: eating! Recently I've found that the push for extended, marble-topped kitchen counters and light-filled dining rooms has

> become overwhelming, when the reality is that most of us are living with perfectly functional (if not strictly trendy) spaces to bash a meal together and feed people. Shifting your attention from the *place* (the beautiful kitchen and dining room you don't have) to the *activity* (eating a lovely meal with people you care about) means you're focusing on creating an experience which is within your control. I think back to my father in that rental house with all the maddening restrictions of a kitchen designed by someone with no soul, and know that he still put delicious meals on the table seven nights a week. We certainly didn't need the latest range-cooker and Shaker cabinet fronts to gather and eat as a family.

Likewise, I can tell you that one of my best experiences was a surprise dinner party I threw for my husband on his birthday a couple of years ago. I over-invited without thinking through the logistics of where people would sit until my daughter had finally gone to bed and I was half an hour away from the first guest arriving. Cue a minor freak-out, swiftly followed by a self-directed pep talk at the stove and then just unabashed joy at having all these gorgeous friends turn up to celebrate with us. I made a kilo of pasta puttanesca, wrote decorative name cards to double down on my insane seating arrangement, opened some good bottles of red and sang 'Happy Birthday' over the lopsided but generously iced chocolate cake. I have a photo from that night, all of us stuffed around the table with big smiles and full glasses. It always makes me feel fuzzy-happy when I look at it.

All of us can bring together some good food, play a little music, light some candles and borrow some extra chairs, if needed, or sit on cushions on the floor. If the vibes are good, no one will care, least not remember, if your cabinets are the latest viral colour or if your oven is from the seventies. Take a picture. Remember these experiences. You've just demonstrated agency over your environment. That's what control feels like.

Some of the sharpest reflections I've heard on the topic of control came from a small group of people I met while conducting the 2017 IKEA research. We ended up calling this cohort 'Home Pioneers' because they lived in ways that might feel like a stretch to the rest of us. One person lived in a dome-shaped eco-house in the middle of the Russian wilderness. Another lived in an empty loft apartment in Tokyo with nearly all his possessions locked up in storage. They were a funny lot, in terms of both eccentricity and good humour. They spanned ages and lifestyles, income and education, but they had one unifying quality – their propensity to actively and regularly change their home environment. As one Home Pioneer from Germany put it: 'I can't let my house take control of me. I've lived all over the world in many houses, so I'm used to doing this. It doesn't scare me. Life throws you curveballs, you have to adapt to them.'

What these people all possessed was drive. It's something I've long been curious about. Why do some people push ever-onwards, whilst others tread water where they are? When we sampled this tendency in our research, we found that people with 'drive' represent a much smaller percentage of the population – around one in four people – compared with the majority, at 60 per cent, who are 'drifters'. When it comes to life at home, drivers are usually excited to experiment with their home environment and embrace change, compared to drifters, who feel uncertain about what change means and prefer stability. At first, this distinction felt like the key to the solution – surely, those of us who struggle with control and change could look to the people with drive and see what we can learn from them. But when I looked closer, I realized that people with drive aren't always changing their home environment. Their feeling of control comes from a much deeper point of recognition within themselves – that they are *capable* of creating change. They believe in their agency. They know they have choices, big or small, whether they exercise them or not. Now I can see that drive is what my parents have. It's the thing that kept them sane for the two years we lived under the tyranny of The Deposit. This perfectly captures why it's possible to experience control where you live, no matter whether you own your home or not, or if you lack the time, money, skills or permission to change so much as a lightbulb.

In this chapter I've encouraged you to ask yourself plenty of questions as a way to explore the feeling of control. Now I'd like to ask you one more as part of your overall reflection:

> → If, with a snap of your fingers, you could change one thing about the way you live in your home, what would it be?

It's a question that allows you to approach change from the opposite direction. Rather than waiting for ways to change your environment so you can change your actions, change your actions so your environment changes around you. To offer up my own kind of Serenity Prayer for us all: when you know your own power, Lord knows what you're capable of.

3

Security

'The ache for home lives in all of us. The safe place where we can go as we are and not be questioned.'

Maya Angelou, All God's Children Need Travelling Shoes

ASK ANYONE WHETHER THEY FEEL secure where they live and their mind will invariably jump to the presence of locks, alarms, curtains and videocam doorbells. It is, without doubt, vital to feel secure at home, given that this intersects with the nested feelings of safety and resilience. So, it's not surprising to hear that 17 per cent of people globally say things like strong locks and bars on the windows make them feel most secure at home. At first glance, defining the feeling of security as feeling 'safe' is helpful in establishing a baseline for this fundamental emotion. Certainly, we all know what it's like to be in spaces and places that feel unsafe, whether that's because of a real threat to our well-being or a perceived one. And all too many of us have had that experience of walking through the streets late at night, keys primed in our hand, and the rush of relief as we shut the door on the outside world and turn to our sanctuary within.

I want to start out by saying that everyone should feel that their home is their sanctuary. But I know from the research that, during the pandemic, when billions of us were confined to our homes, as many as one in five said they didn't feel that way. Security plays a big part in creating a sanctuary, but there can be many complex, and sometimes frightening, reasons to feel unsafe and therefore insecure at home. The stability of our relationships, the physical safety of our possessions and ourselves, and our ability to freely express our identity, to name a few – when these are volatile, under threat or place a danger to our well-being, then nowhere that houses us under these terms can ever feel like home.

I flag this because it would be irresponsible to talk about the feeling of security without acknowledging the deeply insecure situations in which many people – primarily women, children and people within minority groups – are living today. However, there are whole books and tireless campaigns which do a far better job of elaborating on these profound challenges than I ever could in a single chapter. For that reason, I won't focus on the very sharp end of this issue. Rather, I want to discuss an aspect of security that we've all experienced.

Let's start with the fundamental notion of security as a feeling of safety, and then widen the lens. In the IKEA *Life at Home* research, we address security as the matter of *protecting what we care about*. The emotional gap in this case is 24 per cent, which is the smallest out of the eight emotional needs from our home. Still, security is one of the top three needs we have from the home in order of importance. Security is about safety and protection, but it's also about more than that – it's about boundaries. When we feel secure in our home, in our relationships and in our roles in life, it's because we nurture the boundary between our external and our internal selves.

One of the best examples of boundary setting is the act of ensuring privacy. Successfully establishing privacy at home is a significant contributor to whether we feel secure there. It's interesting, then, that only four in ten people believe their home provides enough privacy for those living in it. Privacy is something that feels like a fundamental right, but our access to it is often dependent on the people around us, which makes it tough to maintain. And it's a complicated request. Asking your family or flatmates for some 'alone-time' might make them feel hurt or set off some alarm bells. No wonder one in five people are afraid that someone will take it personally if they ask for privacy, and just over one in ten don't even feel they have the *right* to request it. But request it we must, because privacy at home is essential to our overall health and well-being, given that we need it to achieve some fundamental goals, from properly resting to planning our future. And I've learned this the hard way.

*

I have a sign hanging on the bedroom door – one of only four doors in our apartment – which I can flip between asking for solitude or for hugs, but it's not always spotted by my busy husband or my illiterate children. It's not their fault. Non-verbal signals are never as effective as speaking your truth. But even if we know this is the case, we'll often defer to the non-verbal way out: as many as one in ten people admit they've hidden from their housemates to get some alone-time. I would know – I once spent weeks avoiding one particularly privacy-averse individual in an experience I'll never forget.

When I was twenty, I moved to Arizona in the southwestern United States for a year-long study-abroad programme arranged by my university. I'd never been to America before, but I'd dreamed of it for a long, long time. (Although, I'll admit that those dreams didn't typically play out in the baking heat of the Sonoran Desert, where my new university was located.) This being the early days of the internet, I found accommodation by calling the university administrators, who gave me a bunch of random email addresses for people who had spare rooms. Trisha was the only person to get back to me, and we agreed that I'd take the other half of her bedroom – sight unseen – in what amounted to a two-bed, four-person apartment a ten-minute walk from campus. Now I would be partaking in my bedtime rituals with a woman I'd exchanged only a handful of emails with. But this would turn out to be the least of my problems.

In her emails, Trisha had mentioned two other

flatmates: Fiona, a practising Mormon, and Kim, whom she described simply as 'interesting'. Turns out that living with Kim wasn't just 'interesting' – it was nerve-shredding. Kim repeatedly lied about her age, letting us believe she was twenty-one before a slip of the tongue revealed she was actually in her forties. That was the first red flag. A week after I arrived, I realized she was listening to my phone calls. I was reliant – as most of us were in the early 2000s – on the landline, and we had two handsets to our open-plan kitchen-living room, on to which our bedrooms faced. The phone pinned to the kitchen wall was marginally closest to the room I shared with Trisha. Desperate for privacy, I'd pull the kitchen phone cord as far as it would go, its coils stretched taut across the counter and under my bedroom door when Trisha was out. Then I'd eat a late breakfast from my position on the floor whilst I chatted to my parents back in England and listened sorrowfully as they prepared dinner. I could feel life at home reverberating through the earpiece, and it made me so homesick I thought I would vomit.

One day I heard a faint *click*, like a receiver being picked up somewhere, and the muffled rush of a hand over the mouthpiece. I threw open the bedroom door to see Kim clutching the living room phone to her ear. She looked at me and started laughing in a high and exasperated way that suggested that I was not in on her joke.

After that, she started hiding my groceries. Bunches of bananas turned up in the bookcase. My bread appeared in the cleaning cupboard. Whenever I confronted her, she would start shrieking with laughter. Often, I didn't even need to speak to her – I'd find her watching me from the other side of the room, and eye contact alone set her off into a paroxysm of hysterics. The experiences began to feel so trippy that I wondered if she was slipping LSD into my water at night as part of a hazing ritual. After a chance conversation revealed she couldn't swim, I took to studying for class in the apartment complex pool. I'd prop my textbooks up on the side whilst I lurked in the shallow end until my skin started pruning. She still found me, turning up one afternoon in a frilly polka dot swimsuit and an inflatable ring, like a toddler with a death wish.

    I was a mess during those first two, tender months of my time abroad, trying to make new friends in this bewildering and blisteringly hot place, never knowing if my provisions would be where I'd left them when I woke up. I didn't feel safe and secure, so I didn't feel free. And freedom was the reason I'd packed my rucksack and got on that plane in the first place.

    Living with Kim was at the extreme end of things, but I'd wager that you've experienced similar situations at some point in your own homemaking journey. An overly curious flatmate or parent walking into your bedroom without knocking, perhaps; a partner who keeps asking you questions when you're trying to read something; a child pestering you for snacks when you need to focus on work; and so on. Of course, you might not initially consider these transgressions to be about privacy, though the intrusion has the same effect each time: you were in your own world, and someone entered uninvited.

Establishing privacy at home is so profoundly connected to how we establish ourselves in the world that 70 per cent of people say privacy is important for establishing time and space for activities that enable personal growth. We seem to know on a visceral level what privacy feels like when it's lost – a combination of acute frustration and anxiety – yet we struggle to ask for privacy in terms that capture what we actually need. This may have something to do with the language of privacy – that it tends to evoke images of solitude and shameful secrets behind locked doors and 'no entry' signs. Think about it: when someone you live with asks for some privacy, the first question that comes to mind is usually: *What are they doing in there?* And if you're generally anxiety-prone, like me, it's usually followed by: *Why don't they like me any more?* Which is ridiculous, because we know what we're up to in our own private moments and it's usually something as mundane as staring at our phone or having a shower without our child barging in. All we need is a moment to recentre ourselves, stop the noise and focus inwards. Sometimes we just want to pee in peace. In language we're all familiar with: privacy is not about you, it's about me.

So how do we right this wrong? When we ask for privacy or seek it out, we need three things to happen:

- **A mutual appreciation that something is a private moment**
  Privacy is often individual but it's dependent on others.
- **Getting into the right mindset wherever we are**
  Privacy might require a physical space, but it's always in your head.
- **Achieving something that benefits us**
  Privacy is an action, not a status.

This reframing of privacy, away from solitude and secrets, and towards the everyday needs of happy cohabitation, and good health and well-being, makes it much easier to ask for what we need and more likely that we all get it. This way, it's possible to establish privacy and nurture the feeling of security in any kind of situation – even if you've found yourself living with Kim.

I'd like to propose three actionable, 'hands and heart' approaches to putting in place the foundation for effective privacy at home. Unlike the actions in the previous chapters, these steps are interdependent and sequential, which means we need to take them in order, starting with the hardest.

1. Ask for what you need

Let's begin by addressing the fact that the vast majority of us struggle to get the privacy we need at home because we live with other people. Layered on to this are a few variables that will shape our norms and expectations around privacy, depending on our personal situation. One of them is culture, namely whether you live in a place where individual privacy is lost to the needs of a collective society. This plays out at national and political levels (where people living in China might have different views on privacy compared with people living in Germany, for example), but it can also exist in hyperlocal situations, such as within a housing association or a particularly friendly street with a dedicated and lively WhatsApp group. Another variable is income, where the desire for privacy intersects with the ideals of a home, and people are left feeling that privacy is aspirational because they cannot afford to live where they want. That may explain why 26 per cent of people in the UK and the US feel they don't have enough money to attain privacy. However, it remains the case that the biggest challenges to getting privacy are, by far, the relationships we have and the roles we play at home.

Unsurprisingly, the more people you live with, the harder it is to get privacy. There's the simple matter of available space, and whether it's possible to close a door, for example. But more people also means more competing needs. It's almost certainly why one in three people who live in multi-generational households use work as an excuse to get some alone-time, compared with just one in five people on average. And 81 per cent of people who live with strangers say they need to shut a door to achieve privacy, compared with 69 per cent of people on average. In terms of our roles and identities at home, those who are caregivers – whether it's for children or other dependent family members – are the least likely to get the privacy they need. In fact, caregiving is cited as the number one barrier to privacy around the world, most notably by parents, of whom 50 per cent say that caring for others is the biggest challenge they face in establishing alone-time. Again, this shouldn't be surprising, but it's important to state it for the record. When we identify a challenge and properly name it, we can start finding solutions.

I'm one of those parents who struggles to find alone-time. I also feel that privacy has become aspirational, given that I can't shake the feeling that if we lived in a bigger home, it would be easier for me to remove myself from my in-house wrecking crew every now and then. But I know the solution isn't to leave my family or move home, because I also know that intrusion isn't something that only multiple-occupancy households struggle with. People who live alone talk about the challenges of having to be digitally available, and of the eyes, ears and noises of neighbours. It turns out the solution for more privacy is both one of the easiest and hardest we have to contend with: we have to speak to people and tell them what we need and want. That's why **establishing boundaries** and **setting expectations** is the first step in creating the best preconditions for privacy at home.

I'm sorry, I know this is hard to hear. No one wants to be told that the way through a really sticky problem is *talking it out*. Most of us would rather eat glass than ask the people we see every day to leave us alone. What if they get offended? What if they start doubting our relationship? What if, just giving a purely hypothetical example here, they are four years old and have a screaming meltdown because you dared to shut the bathroom door and don't have a single atom of energy left to hold your boundary? I know how difficult it is to speak plainly on the topic of privacy, having skirted the issue during many years of cohabitation, and I know it's harder for some people than for others. People under twenty-four years old find it harder to ask for privacy than those over fifty-five. Parents of young children find it harder than parents with kids over the age of twenty. In fact, parents of young children are more likely to look at their phones or laptops as a way of saying they need privacy, compared with the global average. Of course, it's not just parents. People of all stripes are more inclined to use non-verbal cues that they want privacy than ask for it. Things like putting headphones on, doing a chore, looking at a device, opening a book, getting up and walking to a different part of the home, avoiding eye contact – be honest, how many of these things have you done? And how effective were they?

The data in the IKEA *Life at Home* Report 2019, which is a deep dive into privacy, are pretty compelling on this, seeing as 'asking outright for privacy' is cited as the most effective method (successful in 81 per cent of cases). Non-verbal actions quickly fall down the ranks; 'looking at a phone' is effective just 52 per cent of the time. But do you know what the least effective strategy is? Dropping hints. That's just 48 per cent effective, the lowest of all the options the research considers. I know you thought you could avoid it, but you can't. This is the simple truth: we have to put on our big-girl and -boy pants and ask for privacy out loud, in terms that are unequivocal.

I now consider myself a veteran of this approach, pockmarked by the scars of poorly understood requests and misunderstandings between roommates and partners. I know how desperate it can feel to offer up a plea for privacy and see it go unheeded, mentally playing back the inevitable argument that erupted as a result and getting wound up all over again. I've been the one in three people who say they feel anxious when they don't get enough privacy and amongst the six in ten women who say they feel frustrated. Which is just to say, *I get it*.

So, I'd like to give you some **conversational primers**, applicable to different situations, to help you on your way. I did not attempt any of these things when I was living with Kim, but years of training means I draw on them weekly with my family. The following are intended for conversations between adults, but afterwards I'll give my pennyworth on how to negotiate privacy with small children.

> **Establish the need for a conversation:**
>
> → If you live with flatmates, **suggest a time** when everyone can get together. Tell them you have something you'd like to discuss which will be beneficial for everyone. Maybe

bring some snacks – people don't revolt on a full stomach.

→ If you live with your partner or family members, **initiate the conversation when you are feeling calm and rested**, and not – as is often the case – at the point when you really need some privacy and there's a good chance you'll flip out.

Frame the discussion:

→ Use a **'both / and' approach** to the topic, by talking about the benefits that come *both* from getting together *and* spending time apart. You want to position privacy as a win-win (which it is), not a trade-off (which it can definitely feel like).

→ Tee up the need for privacy using **clear language,** like: 'Making sure we have time and space for privacy at home is really important for our health and well-being. That's why I'd like to chat about how we can all / both get some alone-time whenever we need it.'

Provide clear examples as a point of reference:

→ Talk about what **spontaneous** moments of privacy currently look like for you, like: 'When I'm reading, I don't want to chat,' or

'When the bathroom door is shut, I don't want you to barge in without knocking.'

→ Talk about what **planned** moments of privacy could look like for you, for example: 'I'd like to chill out for half an hour on my own before cooking dinner,' or 'I'd like the apartment to myself for a morning so I can get some chores done / sing along to theatrical showtunes in drag.'

→ Talk about the times you want to **share a private moment** with other people, whether they live with you or not, for example: 'I'd like to veg out on the sofa and watch trash TV with you when the kids have gone to bed,' or 'I'd like to invite my partner / friends over for dinner. Please can we agree on an evening when I can use the kitchen so we can enjoy our meal without you hovering near by?'

Get some reinforcements:

→ Suggest a **recurring moment** each day / week / month which is blocked out for you to have some privacy, and put it in your calendar. Even better, put it in *their* calendar. Scheduling privacy makes it easier to stick to and harder for others to ignore.

→ Ask for **help** securing the privacy you need, especially if you have children. More

- often than not, another caregiver will need to entertain the kids whilst you get some alone-time. You might need to spell this out for them.

- Reiterate the importance of privacy by being **proactive** about the needs of other people you live with, for example by asking: 'What do you like to do when you have some downtime?' or 'How can I help you catch a break?'

Don't apologize:

- Promise me you will not apologize for asking for privacy – you have nothing to be sorry about. But it's always nice to say thank you.

If you live with small children who have selective hearing and zero boundaries, it might feel overwhelming – if not impossible – to attempt to have a conversation with them about privacy. I have a friend who said she used to hide in her wardrobe to get a minute's break from her kids, until it inadvertently became a thrilling game of hide-and-seek for them. I'm not a parenting expert – just white-knuckling it over here – but there are some wonderful resources on how to create and enforce boundaries with children of all ages that I would suggest looking at, if this has become a struggle for you. A great place to start is the work of Dr Becky Kennedy and her bestselling book, *Good Inside*. When it relates to privacy, remember that kids need privacy too. They need it for the same reasons we do, for their health and well-being. This is a helpful starting point for any conversation you try to have with them about why you need to be alone. If you can connect with them about their feelings, it'll make it easier for them to relate to yours.

Finally, I want to return to an idea I raised earlier – that you can live alone and still struggle with privacy. Sure, the data confirm that people who live alone are most likely to have their privacy needs met, but it's not a done deal. The most egregious challenge is the relentless rise of our 'always on' digital culture, which makes it much harder to draw lines around when we can be contacted, both at work and at play. Not replying to work emails in the evening is one thing, but not replying to multiple texts from your partner is a whole other minefield. The same conversational primers above apply here: frame the need and give concrete examples. People might still get wobbly when you ask for your privacy, but if you can show them how much you care about and invest in the time you are together, it should leave them with no doubt during the time you're apart.

2. Open the door

With the request made, we can turn to our environment to help us feel secure in body and mind. People aside, there are plenty of other factors in the home which can help or hinder privacy, such as noise, smells and light. The more control we have over our home environment (see Chapter 2), the easier it will be to attain privacy when we get the chance. This is particularly important given that the majority of people say they get privacy as-and-when, compared with the 35 per cent who plan for it.

As with all the emotions we experience at home, no one can tell you to feel secure. So it goes for privacy. No one can say, 'Here, I'm giving you some privacy!' and you just magically feel it. Only you, and you alone, will know if what you have is a private moment. You will know it in a place that's hard to locate, but I like to think of it as the door between your exterior world and your interior one. Privacy opens a temporary portal between these worlds – as impermanent as fog – and for as long as it's there, you're able to take yourself into your interior world and wander around freely. But the moment something disturbs your exterior world, like a noise or someone interacting with you, the door disappears. When we feel insecure in our living conditions, this door can never open up. That remains the case even if we feel safe where we live but cannot control our environment. I cannot imagine how unbearable it must be to exist only in the exterior world and never have the chance to retreat to your interior world. This is ultimately what I mean when I talk about having boundaries.

To give your portal the best possible chance of opening up, and for you to maintain that boundary, you need to consider two levels to your environment:

- **The practical things** which make you feel safe and secure at home
- **The sensory things** which make it easier to move into your interior world

Practical but simple things include putting locks on appropriate doors and drawers, and blinds or curtains on windows. You may also want to consider the technology you have in your home, how you interact with it, who else has access to it and what it contains which feels personal or private. One of the most devastating realities of room-sharing in that apartment in Arizona was that I couldn't lock the bedroom door. It felt weird between me and Trisha for a few days before we discussed our needs and found a good flow for how we used the room separately and together. But Kim would just walk in without knocking, multiple times a day. I can attest that dropping hints doesn't work, because even when I told her I was going to bed, she would linger in the doorway. Once, I found her rooting through my wardrobe and the following day she mentioned something over breakfast that strongly suggested she had been reading my private journal. When I asked her, she laughed like a hyena. I cannot express how utterly intolerable the whole situation was.

Do what you must, in practical terms, to give yourself peace of mind. I'm aware that privacy in relation to our online activity at home is a fast-moving and complex issue, and I don't have the capacity or the knowledge to cover that here. I'm also not going to tell you that you can feel secure through willpower alone, because it's not helpful or realistic. Whilst privacy is a mental state, it always requires the intimate cooperation of our physical spaces. As I discussed in the previous chapter, making changes to our environment and being in control feels harder when you rent, but there will always be options which get you closer to what you need. I was so messed up by my living situation that I never even thought to ask if we could have a lock on the bedroom door, so take this as permission to ask your landlord to install one, if you need it. Upgrade your flimsy curtains to fitted blinds. Get a lockbox for your personal keepsakes. Do what you need to cover the basics so you can focus on the rest.

When it comes to our senses, thankfully there's so much more to play with. We want to take steps towards privacy that align with what we can hear, see, smell, taste and touch at home, to get our heads into the right frame of mind for a private moment. I think of these steps as **privacy enhancers**. Here are five great privacy-enhancing questions about your living situation:

> → What can you **hear?** Does the noise compete with your needs or does it help you? What soundscape options could you tap into, such as playing music or white noise, wearing noise-reduction headphones, opening the windows to hear birdsong or closing them to muffle the sound of traffic?

→ What can you **see**? How does the light make you feel? Do you find it easier to get what you need with daylight or cosy nightlights? What's around you, and does it compete with your needs or help you? Consider visual disturbances, such as clutter on the desk when you want to focus, or a pile of laundry in the bathroom when you want to soak in the tub.

→ What can you **smell**? Is there a particular scent that's going to charge things up for you? Is fresh air the key to privacy, or do you want a perfumed candle? Are there obnoxious smells which make it hard to get into your headspace, like lingering odours from food or pets?

→ Is **taste** part of your privacy experience? Do you want to consume something when you have a moment to yourself? What are your comfort foods? Is there a particular drink that helps you get into the right headspace, like a freshly brewed coffee or a cocktail on ice?

→ What do you want to **feel** on your body? Are there textures and fabrics which help with privacy, through clothing or textiles? Do you need to sit or do you want to move around?

Does your home make it easy to answer these questions? I imagine there are things you could easily do to get your senses better aligned with your privacy needs. It's rare that I get alone-time at home with two kids, so I try to make the most of the precious hours after they go to bed. The first thing I do is remove all the 'hard' clothing I'm in (bra, jeans, etc.) and put on clothes which have a high elasticity count. Then I'll take out my contact lenses, remove my make-up and pull up my hair. I'll pop on the kettle or pour a glass of wine, fix a little chocolatey-nibbly snack, settle at the end of the sofa with the reading light and crack open a magazine or a book. If this moment coincides with the evenings my husband goes to the gym, all the better because then I can watch reruns of *Gilmore Girls* or some *Housewives* franchise without having to explain why. That's when I feel it – that portal opening up – and I leave the physical space I'm in and connect with myself. It's not foolproof, because more often than not one of my children will wake and bleat for something just as soon as I've settled, and that portal will close again. But I cherish the times I get the privacy I need when I've had a rough run of things and need to retreat.

The optimal place for privacy, of course, is your own home, simply because it's easier to control the environment around you, and establish a feeling of security, compared with public spaces. But there will be many instances in your homemaking journey when it's just impossible to get what you need within your own four walls, and you'll seek privacy beyond the front door. One in ten people globally say they get privacy the most from being outdoors in nature, especially people who live in multiple-occupancy households. This was evidently my situation when I lived with Kim, and thankfully I was blessed with the wild landscape of Arizona and its iconic Saguaro cacti to get some 'me-time'. I'd never so much as rambled a day in my life before then, but suddenly I found myself with a frenzied interest in the university hiking club, which culminated in a two-day trek to the bottom of the Grand Canyon and back. You can get a lot of privacy down there.

The reality is that life at home is a porous thing, and the feeling of home can be found in spaces and places beyond your address. It will always be true that home should be ideally placed to meet all your emotional needs, and that we all deserve to feel at home where we live – but when we don't, we'll continue to reach into our neighbourhood cafes, streets and parks (or UNESCO World Heritage sites, in my case) to get what we need. I see this time and again amongst people who cannot get privacy at home. And it's why I don't mind doing a last-minute dash to the supermarket for ingredients, because it guarantees me at least twenty minutes away from the chaos of my family life, and I can zone out amongst all the produce. That magical portal can open up in all kinds of places, even the fruit-and-veg aisle.

3. Do the right thing

Once our conversations have been conducted and our senses are aligned, we can turn to the main event. What do we want to *do* when we finally get a break?

One of the most important things to know about privacy is that it's not a status, but an action. More to the point, **privacy is an enabler** – a tool for unlocking significant benefits for our body and mind. Even if we use our private moments to do absolutely nothing more fitful than sleep, we're still choosing to do *something*.

> Broadly speaking, there are four kinds of well-being benefits to privacy and they sit on a spectrum from low- to high-energy:
>
> * At the lower end, privacy is a way to **recover** and **relax**, such as lying down in a quiet room, napping or doing a little pampering and self-care. At the higher end, privacy is a way to **focus** and **play**, such as accomplishing some tasks, writing in a journal or having a dance party.

These activities are what we do when we're able to open that door between our external and internal worlds, and the benefits we get are fundamental to our overall health and well-being. They enable us to gather energy when we are tired, regulate our systems when we're firing on all cylinders, calm our minds when we're strung out, and connect with the people we love. That's why 97 per cent of people (yes, you read that right) say they do specific activities when they have privacy at home. If we perpetually operate in our outside world, plagued with distraction and intrusion, and never have the chance to reap the benefits from being in our internal world, we become like an empty eggshell – brittle to the touch. We lose the softest parts of ourselves. This is why three in four people agree that privacy is fundamental to their well-being. I shouldn't even need to give you the data to make this point, because you *know* it deep down inside already.

On any given day, we may want to tap into all of these benefits, depending on our energy levels and needs, which is why we want the groundwork in place so we can get to the good stuff as quickly as possible. The factors which enable privacy to happen are interconnected, meaning that how you frame your request and set the mood will be shaped by the activity you intend to do. The kind of set-up you need for a four-hour binge-athon of your favourite TV shows is going to be different to the conversation and space you need to get a bit of life admin done that's been hanging over you for six months. Knowing what you truly need from your privacy makes it easier to establish your boundaries, and you get to the benefits much quicker. If you've found yourself banging heads with your partner or your flatmates over this issue, it might be that one of you is looking for privacy to lie down in a dark room and disconnect after a hellish week, and the other wants to plan that holiday you've been discussing for months.

Whilst the activities may vary in energy and intention, there is one trait that connects them all: they are things we choose to do because we do not want to be *judged* whilst we do them. When we get privacy, no one can judge the content of our diary or the messages sent to friends or lovers; no one can review our performance as we sing along to our favourite songs or dance with our kids; no one can question the way we sleep or soothe, or what we choose to watch on TV. No one can give any kind of opinion on what we find when we enter our interior world. It's this aspect of privacy which is the most important benefit of all – when we are free from judgement, we are free to be ourselves.

So, ask yourself: *What would you do if you suddenly had one hour of alone-time today?*

Now that you know that privacy is an action, think as broadly as possible about all the things you might do in that moment. This is your go-to list the next time you get that hour of alone-time for real.

You might be wondering what happened with Kim. Well, things inevitably came to a head after a few months of unbearable coexistence. I can't recall a specific event that caused this; more that each intrusion was like a shovelful of sand and before long we all found ourselves buried and suffocating. Kim headed out of the apartment one morning to go to her lectures, and the three of us remaining finally said the quiet part out loud: *We. Need. To. Move.* With the apartment superintendent's help, we broke our lease, signed a new one for an apartment in the same complex and moved in a week later. I'd like to say we did it with kindness to Kim, but we literally moved our bags when she was at lectures because we were too terrified to tell her in person. She found out soon enough, of course, and came banging on our front door to demand access. I was alone in the apartment that afternoon, and stood with my back against the door for twenty hair-raising minutes as she raged on the pavement outside. Finally, spent and defeated, she walked away only to return ten minutes later to slide a homemade 'Notice of Legal Action' under the door, written and wildly misspelt using a variety of colourful crayons. I'm no lawyer, but I was pretty confident a sheet of A4 with angry faces drawn on it had no legally binding consequences.

When the dust settled in the new apartment, with flatmates who understood and maintained boundaries and privacy, my life opened up. I had originally moved to America because I wanted to step away from the labels that had been placed upon me after years of following an expected path. I wanted freedom. Finally feeling secure in my home, I found it abundantly easier to be brave and try new things. I wrote for the local paper, I hosted a radio show, I took classes in storytelling and film; I performed in musicals and sang in a choir; I hiked mountains and canyons and took aqua aerobics and Pilates and jazz-dance lessons. And, yes, I partied and drank warm beer out of those iconic American red plastic cups and got pulled over by the police whilst sitting in the back of an SUV and showed them fake ID. I travelled, too – across Arizona to California and Nevada, and then all the way down through Central America to Costa Rica. By the time I took my flight home, I was profoundly changed. And I knew how to protect the things I cared about.

When we feel secure in our life at home, we are able to move freely between our internal and external worlds. In certain kinds of light, feeling secure might suggest a hardening – that it's about resistance to volatility and disruption – but I think that feeling secure is a softening. That softening is seen in the way we let our guard down and open the door to our inner life at home. Listening to our own voice requires a certain tenderness.

As you reflect on what privacy enables you to do in your own life at home, and how intimately it relates to your well-being, lean into that softening. **What would you do if no one was watching? Who would you be without the fear of being judged? And how far away from these answers are you today?**

By cultivating effective privacy in your own life at home, you can close that emotional gap. That's the remarkable thing about a little alone-time – it helps us be secure *in* ourselves, not just be *by* ourselves.

4

Accomplishment

'To be yourself in a world that is constantly trying to make you something else is the greatest accomplishment.'

Ralph Waldo Emerson

WHEN I GOT BACK FROM Arizona, to start my final undergraduate year at Edinburgh University, I was so mellowed by the desert heat that I had forgotten what it was like to live in the Scottish capital. The Scots have some fantastic words for things that feel acutely of their terrain, including the marvellously onomatopoeic word *dreich*, which means miserable or depressing. It is most often used to describe their weather. And it was a truly *dreich* day when I signed the lease on my new apartment – a fourth-floor walk-up just off the historic Royal Mile that had plenty of charm and no central heating.

To pay my eyewatering rent for this nineteenth-century icebox, I worked as a historical-character-reenactment tour guide in an underground complex of hidden streets bordering the Royal Mile itself. The morning I arrived for my first shift I was assigned the character role of 'Jonet', the fancy daughter of a wealthy merchant, and taken into a dank basement where I was given an ill-fitting replica seventeeth-century frock and bonnet to wear. The tours were scripted but I was encouraged to add my own ad libs and personal touches once I 'got in touch with Jonet's personality'. This was a tough ask, given that the material was pretty thin on backstory and motivation, and leant very heavily on a handful of jokes about chucking toilet water out of the window. It soon became clear that nearly all the employees were 'resting actors' who were kicking their heels between drama studies and performance gigs. They lapped up the scripts, honing accents and personality quirks until it wasn't entirely clear where the character ended and the employee began. One guy was so 'method' that he made his own leather boots and carried a real sword. I felt like a fraud, but it was better pay (and considerably better hours) than pulling pints, so I got stuck in.

I worked that gig all year, six hours a day, five days a week, in between my studies. It didn't take long before I knew the script back to front and upside down, and could conduct vast parts of the tour in full character whilst simultaneously thinking about my to-do list. When I hung my costume up each day, I carried a tired satisfaction, and a few pound coins from tips, knowing I'd done a good job. By that point I was writing my final degree thesis, so when I wasn't larking about underground I was reading and writing at home or in the library. As autumn edged into winter, the *dreich* weather started to bite through the thin walls of the apartment and my bones ached. My flatmate and I shared a single heater on wheels that we'd roll from room to room, depending on who was in greater need. I tapped away on an old and wheezing second-hand computer which took so much energy to run that the plastic casing was warped from radiated heat. If I sat close enough, I could warm my face whilst I typed.

And that was how it went, for the most part. By day, I'd doff my bonnet to hundreds of tourists, and in the evenings I'd change into four layers of thermal clothes and fingerless gloves, eking out my thesis, line by line, before shuffling into my stone-cold bed. By the end of the academic year, I'd managed to pay my rent on time every month and get my degree with first-class honours. Doing these things in parallel taught me that accomplishing things – getting shit done – is not a talent but a discipline. It's a muscle you have to exercise through repetition and routine, just like the script I delivered more times than I can count. Any time I feel like I can't do something, I think back to that strange year and feel the muscle twitching.

The IKEA *Life at Home* research shows that, of all the emotional needs we have at home, accomplishment has the biggest emotional gap – with a whopping 39 per cent gulf between importance and reality. It's actually a relatively new phenomenon, this desire to feel accomplishment at home, a likely consequence of the Covid-19 pandemic, when home had to do and be more for so many people. Looking at our behaviours and feelings across the darkest days of the pandemic, 2020–2022, the need to feel accomplishment was something people started talking about for the first time during the (virtual) IKEA home visits in 2021, and the surveys behind the IKEA *Life at Home* Report only began tracking it in 2022.

The rise of remote and flexible working has got something to do with this development, creating a new context for our daily lives in which many different kinds of things are achieved in a domestic setting which might previously have been realized elsewhere. But I don't want to conflate working with accomplishment. When people talk about accomplishing things in their lives and how home should enable them to do this better, they are not – for the most part – talking about doing their jobs better. In some ways, we've created a bit of a distraction for ourselves on this matter. At the peak of the pandemic, millions of knowledge-economy workers around the world began to work from home – first out of necessity, then increasingly out of comfort and common sense. But the long periods of lockdown also unearthed a wide array of other activities that people wanted to do from home, like baking bread or practising yoga, which continued when we had relative freedom of movement – and even when many of us had to go back to an office again. Data from the *Life at Home* research in 2023 show that as many as one in four people sometimes work from home, which is a sizable proportion of the workforce with the opportunity to tap into more accomplishment during the working day.

It makes sense, of course. I mean, who doesn't love getting shit done? Whether that's sorting out the laundry, weeding the garden, or writing your first book – big or small, we all love the glow of satisfaction that comes from making progress. And the good news is that home is the perfect environment to set us on our way. In fact, one of the legacies of the pandemic is that many of us realized how much *more* we could accomplish at home when we also did our jobs there, rather than squandering valuable time and energy commuting to the office. For those who cracked this oyster open – the people who perfected their sourdough bread or redecorated the living room when they otherwise would have been packed into a train or snarled up in traffic – it felt liberating. These actions and activities were positive contributors to their health and well-being, and clear markers of progress. They could look at their home-baked loaf, for example, and feel a sense of pride at their improved abilities.

However, this opportunity wasn't possible for everyone. For all those who were shaking up new cocktail recipes on Zoom Hangouts with their besties, there were many more barely getting through the day. People with caring responsibilities, health needs, inflexible jobs . . . They were all doing more, too, but it didn't feel much like accomplishment – it felt like hell. On top of this were the reports of increased mental health concerns such as depression and anxiety – something one in four people say they experienced during the first year of the pandemic, according to the *Life at Home* research – which makes doing anything at all feel so much harder. This contrast in experiences captures the essence of accomplishment, which is that it's not about doing more – it's about doing it better.

James Clear, author of the bestselling book *Atomic Habits*, may know this as much as anyone. His work on the topic has transformed my approach to how I define, design and deliver on progress in my own life, thanks to his simple but compelling concept around creating good habits and breaking bad ones. Habits, Clear explains, are behaviours that have become automatic. Good habits are the things we do without even thinking which help us learn, grow and connect. Bad habits are the behaviours which hold us back. As Clear puts it, 'the quality of our lives so often depends on the quality of our habits'. One important thing I've learned from my own experiences, and from those of the people included in the *Life at Home* research, is that home is an extraordinary canvas for habit formation and accomplishing things. Almost everything we set out to do on any given day begins or ends at home, creating a profound interplay between where we live and how we make progress in our lives. As Clear explains, the two biggest triggers for habits are location and time, meaning our environment has a greater influence on our individual behaviour than something as intrinsic as motivation. It's easy to see how this can go both ways, given that your home can be the stimulus for both good and bad habits. But the good news, as Clear reminds us, is that 'You don't have to be the victim of your environment. You can also be the architect of it.'

So, how do we design our home to be a bedrock of accomplishment? Insights from several years of *Life at Home* research reveal a few key qualities of the home that lend themselves to the formulation of good habits and routines which help us make progress, namely:

* **Home is where we already occupy ourselves with a significant number of habits that have the potential to improve our lives**
  It's easier to add new habits to existing ones than to start them in isolation.

* **Home is where we can best enjoy privacy and the opportunity to try things without a fear of judgement**
  Good habits are about incremental change, favouring repetition over perfection, which means they thrive well in environments where we are willing and able to fail.

* **When our home reflects our identity, we are more likely to see it as a place that supports our health and well-being**
  And it's our habits that significantly contribute to our identity. This constant feedback loop between space, habit and identity can create a positive spiral towards progress.

Taking these qualities as starting points for my 'hands and heart' approach, I've expanded on some of the most actionable aspects of habit formation and placed them firmly where I believe we all have the best opportunity to make progress: our home.

Zone your home

There's a theory that the secret to a good night's sleep is to start preparing for it the moment you wake up. There are so many interconnected dependencies around getting a solid eight hours' kip that we have to start addressing them as early as possible in the day. In the same spirit, I believe the steps you need to take to create healthy habits and routines always start at home, no matter whether home is where you intend to complete them or not.

Take exercise, for example: you might *decide* to go to the gym four mornings a week to get fitter, but it's more likely that you'll *actually* go if you pull out your gym clothes and fill a water bottle the night before so you're not faffing around first thing. The gym is where you do the exercise, but home is where you set things in motion.

Every single good habit, goal or intention you set for yourself, regardless of its scale or time frame, can start at home. Your home is uniquely positioned to cater to your accomplishment needs because it provides the context for good habit formation as well as an up-and-running system. This is because your home is typically where you greet the day (accounting for sleep-overs and travel, and so on), so it's a regular touchstone for you. And it's also where you already undertake a large variety of habits and routines, most of which you probably don't think twice about – such as getting ready for work, preparing meals and winding down for bed. Reflecting on this duality, I believe one of the first and most impactful things you can do to nurture accomplishment in your life is to **zone your home**, and bring the environment and activity together.

One of the most interesting observations about life at home during the Covid-19 pandemic was that people's perceptions of the 'multi-functional home' soured a little. I suspect it was because many homes were suddenly stretched beyond their reasonable capacity to function on multiple levels. Many rooms felt a bit 'jack of all trades', with no single space ever really delivering brilliantly on any one thing. This mission creep of the home, evidenced through numerous online meetings taken from our beds or aerobics sessions in the front room, meant the spaces we might previously have primed for one important routine in our domestic life (like sleeping or relaxing) were now catering to a mash-up of functions. The result was like eating at a stuff-yourself-silly buffet, where you've got a plate piled high with every different kind of cuisine but everything starts to taste the same. What the *Life at Home* research indicates is that whilst people still need their home to be able to accommodate a wider range of activities than it had before, they want to be clearer about which spaces serve which purpose. This is the difference between a multi-functional home and a multi-purpose home – namely, the difference between *how* something is done in a certain space and *why* it is done there and not somewhere else. When the rooms or spaces in our home have been assigned a clear purpose, we make a deeper connection to our motivating goals and intentions.

Layered on to this are the routines that we already employ in our daily lives throughout our home, whether we observe them as routines or not. Take, for example, the fact that you get up every morning (or afternoon – who am I to judge?), and in the time between opening your eyes and heading out of your front door, you likely perform a litany of things which have become habitual – brushing your teeth, picking out clothes, making breakfast, and so on. You probably don't actively think about these things, you just do them the same way every day. (If you have kids, you're almost certainly more aware of the things you used to do without thinking, like putting your shoes on and leaving the house before you die of old age.) These kinds of automatic actions are fertile ground for inserting new ones which better serve your goals and intentions. This is what James Clear calls 'habit stacking'. This lovely interplay between the environment we're already in and the routines we already enjoy can help us achieve accomplishment.

Now, let's take stock of what it is you ultimately want to work towards, whether that's locking down a recurring activity or realizing a single achievement, and how you can use your home as a springboard for action. Here's an exercise to get you started:

> → **Imagine yourself a year from now** – what activities are you doing or what experiences are you having that make you feel good and proud? Paint that picture in your mind by thinking about where you are, how you feel, who you're with and what you're doing.
>
> → Now isolate the top three things you're doing or experiencing which resonate in that image – these are your **priority progressions**.

If it feels overwhelming to take the long view from scratch, here are the recurrent clusters of goals and ideal elements of the home that emerge in the *Life at Home* research and which you could use as individual prompts for that image:

- Health and well-being
- Rest and relaxation
- Relationships and family
- Finances
- Learning and developing new practical skills
- Career and professional development
- Travel and adventure

Examples of possible activities where you might want to prioritize progress include: saving enough money to go on a luxury holiday at the end of the year; improving your diet and exercise regime so you feel healthier and stronger; starting a creative project to help you express yourself.

Now, you need to assign each of your priority progressions a dedicated space in your home. This is where you can focus your energy on providing yourself with stimulus, encouragement and the wherewithal to take action. It certainly doesn't have to be the only place you make progress towards your goal, but it should operate a bit like an accomplishment 'nerve centre', with good habits underway that charge the rest of your day within and outside of home. There's no set formula for which space will be best suited to your priorities, but to help shape your thinking, I've plotted the three examples I provided above into existing activities and spaces in a typical home:

> → **Saving money for a luxury holiday:** This kind of activity fits into a slate of other things we tend to call 'life admin': paying bills, corresponding with people, managing our responsibilities, etc. Adulting, basically. Doing these things in one particular place at home, like at a desk in the corner of your living room, gives you a clean break between admin and relaxing, so you're not trying to pay your overdue credit card bill from your phone whilst simultaneously bingeing the latest drop on Netflix. It also means you can be specific about the tasks that need to be completed and allocate enough time to sit in that one place each week and do them.

There are also some simple cues you can employ to make you proactively think about your finances – like leaving your wallet on your desk when you're at home (so when you pick it up to go out, you're prompted to think about what your budget is), or tacking up a picture of the place you want to visit as a visual reminder of what you're saving up for.

→ **Improving diet and exercise:** The kitchen is an obvious go-to for this, but you should make it a place that feels nourishing rather than restrictive. This might mean reorganizing your fridge or pantry so the more nutritious options are quickly available when you're grabbing that mid-afternoon snack, and putting your multivitamins next to your coffee machine so you remember to take them first thing. Potted herbs on the windowsill also provide a lovely stimulus for making your own meals as well as that all-important biophilic boost I mentioned in Chapter 2. I've started leaving a huge water bottle on the edge of my kitchen counter, so I'm prompted to hydrate with water, instead of (yet) another cup of tea, whenever I enter the kitchen. Consider the fridge door, too – use those magnets to stick up your workout schedule, the flyer for your favourite yoga class or a photo of you finishing that 5k race as you work towards your first marathon.

→ **Starting a creative project:** If your home is small, sometimes the last thing you want to do is leave new equipment or half-completed projects lying around. These are the moments when we long for that room of one's own, believing that if we *just had the space* we'd be churning out award-winning manuscripts or critically acclaimed podcasts. The reality is that creative projects invariably tend to happen in all kinds of spaces which have other purposes too, or outside of the home, but they must still be anchored where we live. Conversely, I think the bedroom can be a great place for creativity because it's one of the only places we can let our minds wander. I agree with the broad advice that beds should only be used for sleeping and sex, but this misses an opportunity to use that liminal time between snoozing and waking when we can be charged with inspiration. As a writer, my bedside table is piled up with books, which makes me read almost every night before I sleep, and I have a small notebook so I can jot down any thoughts that pop into my head. Hanging on the back of my bedroom door is a floor-length, dusty-pink kimono from a trip to Japan,

> which I wear if I have the chance to write in the mornings before everyone else is up. It's the first thing I see when I get out of bed, and putting it on immediately makes me feel boho and whimsical, like a carefree writer from another era, rather than a tired and crumpled mother staring at her laptop at five in the morning. I encourage you to think laterally about how your bedroom could embrace your creative side. From meaningful artwork to specific objects to items of clothing, this space can provide a daily nudge towards the project you're developing and the person you want to be. It's why I love this line from *Anne of Green Gables*, when Anne is scolded by Marilla that 'Bedrooms were made to sleep in'. Anne replies, 'Oh, and dream in too, Marilla. And you know one can dream so much better in a room where there are pretty things.'

By zoning your home this way, and aligning space with activity, you can establish a powerful foundation for the goals and intentions you set for yourself as you progress through life.

Satisfaction shots

In a 2014 video that went viral, Admiral William H. McRaven told a crowd of graduates during his University of Texas at Austin Commencement Address,

'If you make your bed every morning, you will have accomplished your first task of the day. It will give you a small sense of pride and encourage you to do another task. And another. And another.' Aside from the fact that there are few things as sad as getting into an unmade bed, this is outstanding advice when it comes to creating a path for accomplishment. These regular acts of domestic success, as simple as plumping a pillow, are how we establish the discipline required to accomplish bigger and better things throughout our life. That's why my second tried-and-tested approach to progress is a simple but deeply effective one: **tapping into regular boosts of accomplishment when you need them most.**

We've all had One Of Those Days, when everything seems to go wrong and we psychologically (or actually) lose our way. Hard-fought routines suddenly unravel; the weather ruins our plans; planes, trains and automobiles leave us hanging; promises are broken. Sometimes nothing much of anything happens at all, and we're just waiting for something to shift so we can get our head back in the game. The best way out of these situations is to give yourself a small shot of satisfaction. That simple act will force you out of your spiral of chaos or incompetence and get you back on track. This is how it goes:

> → Think about something you can get done at home in **one minute**, something you can get done in **ten minutes** and something you can do in **one hour**.

> The **one-minute** task is going to be something staggeringly simple, like putting your coffee cup in the dishwasher or yesterday's underwear in the laundry basket.
>
> In **ten minutes**, you can reasonably expect to complete a task with connected parts, like folding the laundry and putting it away, or scrubbing dried toothpaste off the sink and restocking the toilet paper.
>
> In **one hour**, you have the chance to tackle something you've been thinking about for days or weeks, like cleaning out the fridge, putting up a picture, or sorting out your desk drawers.

You know that bit of life admin you've been putting off for months because you can't bring yourself to do it, and then you finally force yourself and it takes literally minutes to complete and feels *so good*? Yeah, that feeling. That's what we're doing here. You're gifting yourself a dose of accomplishment in as little as sixty seconds. You can toggle between the 1:10:1 depending on how your day is going, where your head's at, and what you have capacity for. It works every time.

Group work

In the spring of 2022, a friend of mine who lives locally asked me if I'd like to fix a regular evening to go for a run along the beach with her. We both have kids and full-time jobs, so exercise is one of those things that easily slides unless it's planned and protected. We decided that Wednesdays were best and that, given we were also both members of the local winter-bathing club, afterwards we'd have a dip in the sea then soothe our aching limbs in the sauna. That weekly commitment has created one of the most meaningful experiences in my life, as we head into another year of what we now affectionately call *The Ladies' Run & Dip Club*. We've grown in members and have even celebrated four babies between us in that time. The reason it has endured is because we keep each other accountable.

We don't overcomplicate things. There's just a single chat group which we check every Wednesday to see who can make it that evening. It's an unwritten rule that we don't leave anyone hanging, so if you've said you'll go and there's just one other person joining then you never renege on the commitment at the last minute, no matter what life (or, more likely, the weather) is doing. We've run and bathed in all seasons, through biting winds, lashing rain, snow and hail and – ever so occasionally – perfect, sunset-kissed Danish summer nights. There are countless times when it's the last thing I want to do, but if a friend jumps on to the chat to say she's up for it, then I am too. So often it's the best thing I do all week.

Accountability is about showing up for yourself, even when – no, *especially* when – it's bloody hard. And showing up for yourself is how you progress through life. Sometimes it can feel easier to show up for others, when we regularly put ourselves last, but there's undoubtedly a sweet spot in supporting those around you in an activity that also includes and benefits you. Data from the *Life at Home* research during the Covid-19 pandemic show that, along with the rise of accomplishment in our domestic lives, people reported closer relationships with their families and a greater sense of belonging in their community. Rubbing along with one another, even under duress, can provide the kind of friction that might just trigger a new routine or activity, where your friends, family or housemates provide a built-in accountability network from the get-go.

If accountability is something you struggle with, I want you to think about one or two people in your daily life who could be your accountability partners. Perhaps it's someone you'll invite to join you in your newest hobby or activity; or perhaps it's just a matter of telling your partner or friend that you intend to do something, so they regularly ask how it's going. A writer friend of mine has a get-together every two weeks with another writer, where they exchange five hundred words from their latest drafts and chat about it over beers. Even in a fortnight of slow starts, dead ends and missed opportunities, five hundred words is always doable, especially if someone else is expecting to read it with a cold one.

I promise that if you reach out to those people today and commit to something, you'll immediately notice how much harder it is to avoid making progress.

Progress over perfection

Maybe it's my history degree or the fact that I spent a year in historical costume, but I've always loved the feel of 'period' homes. Give me a hundred-plus years, tall ceilings, wooden floors, beautiful cornicing – it all makes my heart beat faster. When my husband and I bought our apartment, in Copenhagen, we got the keys to a small but charming period property that came with an oddly shaped hallway cupboard that seemed to have missed out on all the renovation work over the previous century. The wallpaper inside looked as old as the building itself, and the shelves were falling off disintegrating plaster with horsehair in it. We shoved our coats, bike helmets and cat food in there and ignored it for years. And then the Covid-19 pandemic hit just as I became a mother, and *all* I could think about was that cupboard.

With the uncertainty of taking care of a baby during a global health crisis churning inside me, I turned my attention to this one thing I could fix. Every evening, when my daughter was finally asleep, I'd quietly take everything out of the cupboard and strip the wallpaper, patch up the holes, prime and paint. I had no idea what I was doing. I had to google 'Will old wallpaper poison me?' and watch YouTube videos about treating woodworm. I cut new shelves from offcuts with a blunt saw in the basement, and painted them using half-empty tubs of emulsion our decorators had left behind. It took me an hour a day for an entire month to complete. When I finally got the new coat-rack up and the job was as done as it could be, I burst into tears. It's no coincidence that the following week, I started jotting down the very first ideas for this book.

I am absurdly proud of that cupboard but I'm not fishing for compliments when I say that it is, at best and objectively speaking, a mediocre patch-up job. Yet I love it because it represents how far you can go when you take things one step at a time and stop worrying about whether you're doing it right. Our homes are generous spaces for safely holding works in progress, be they interiors (like my cupboard) or more transformational dreams for yourself. Where we live should ideally be a welcoming space to try and test, to incrementally move things forward without having to make excuses for how well or how quickly they're going. Working towards meeting your emotional needs of comfort, control and security from the previous chapters will help put in place the foundations for exactly this.

In a culture of toxic productivity and hyper-performance, where people feel the need to squeeze every drop of value from any given hour, I'd like us to take the longer-term view. What I really want is for us to start **celebrating progress, not perfection**, in the things that we're moving towards. There are two parts to this:

- Knowing that the smallest actions are as important as the largest
- Decoupling completion from accomplishment

If you have in mind some good intentions for yourself which have long or uncertain trajectories connected to them – like writing a book or competing in an Iron Man – then the road ahead can feel pretty daunting. That's why I recommend you boil your project down to the smallest possible actions you can take which still support your progress, and assign some form of celebration to them. This might be as simple as speaking kindly to yourself – a well-intentioned 'well done, good job' if you manage to put your trainers on, for example, goes a long way if you are otherwise used to admonishing yourself for doing the bare minimum. When I sit down to write at home, I celebrate with a cup of tea or a small square of chocolate when my time is up, no matter what the word count looks like or how lucid the prose is. My smallest action is simply to 'be in touch with my writing', and some days that might mean I only have enough energy to reread a few paragraphs from the previous day. I celebrate showing up for myself, not for writing 2,000 words a night. By being in touch with my writing every day, I'm always making progress in my work.

Many accomplishments, by nature of the fact that they're about practising good habits, don't have finish lines at all. The kind of actions you might want to take in your life, based on the exercises in this chapter, might be about shifting your lifestyle or attitudes around things such as your finances or health, and then maintaining them. This is progress across a lifetime, with no single moment at which to point the camera and say 'Ta-dah, it's done!' If you're a chronic completer-finisher like me, this might leave you wondering what you have to show for it all if you don't get to tick something off your to-do list. Of course, the first thing I did when I finally finished that godforsaken cupboard was show it off to anyone who looked in my direction, like a child with a new drawing. But other acts of progress in my life, like staying free of credit card debt or finally going to the dentist, are neither Instagram-worthy nor conclusive. I celebrate them nonetheless. *Good job, well done.*

One of the most important reasons to shine a light on the actions we take over the long term, regardless of the outcome, is because they deeply inform our identity. Aristotle said, 'We are what we repeatedly do', reflecting on the power of routine as a building block for how we show up in the world. It's similar to a line a yoga teacher once told me, as I um'd and ah'd over some position rather than trusting my body to move: 'The way we do anything is the way we do everything.' It's not just our projects that are works in progress – we are, too. That's why it's so important to attend to the small actions, because they shape who we are over our lifetime. So, tell your friends and family about your progress, no matter how small or mundane you think it might feel at the time. If you wait for a big reveal at the end, you're missing out on showing them who you're becoming along the way.

It's a curious thing to be writing about the feeling of accomplishment in a manner which is proof positive of the concept. Writing this chapter has provided me with one of the most fertile grounds on which to test my own solutions – often in real time – although I sometimes felt I was the one being tested. Due to my family and work commitments, I don't get many stretches of uninterrupted writing time, so I have to be precise and agile in how I use the precious minutes (and I truly mean minutes) that I get. The fact that this book is in your hands is a result of my doing the first exercise I set you in this chapter, when I established it was one of my top three 'priority progressions', in the summer of 2023. After that, I made writing impossible to resist, talked to close friends and family about it and celebrated every step I took along the way. Writing almost anything, let alone a book, is often an exasperating sequence of fits and starts, wrong turns and dud drafts before you get to something that doesn't make you cringe when you read it back. The only way I was going to get it done was by establishing good domestic routines and taking it line by line, just as I did when writing my degree thesis and learning my tour character's script back in that *dreich* Scottish winter of 2005. The novelist Anne Lamott explains, in her utterly glorious instructional book about writing and life, that the way through anything is no more complicated than taking it step by step, just as her father once instructed her younger brother, who was overwhelmed at the prospect of completing an ornithological project for school: 'Bird by bird, buddy. Just take it bird by bird.'

In this way, I was constantly thinking about my own relationship with accomplishment whilst I was writing about the topic. I was also holding myself to account when I outlined the different ways you can bring more progress into your own life at home. It made me more sympathetic to the fact that many other spaces and places, beyond home, play an important role in how we progress, given that I wrote many of these words sitting in cafes, parks, playgrounds, holiday homes, hotels, trains, airports, the cloakroom at my daughter's dance school and – on one memorable occasion – outside a florist's in a shopping mall because that's where my baby had finally fallen asleep in his pushchair.

There will undoubtedly be many places in your life which also provide this kind of context for accomplishment, from the gym to the library and anywhere in between. This is good. There might be days when it feels like the *only* way you can get anything done for yourself is to leave your home, and this can also be good if it fires you up. Lean into it, get up an hour earlier and go to that yoga class. Or take a book to the park when you have a short break. But maybe you start to resent the lack of space or opportunity at home, and that resentment stops you from doing or trying anything at all. That needs addressing. Here, I want to encourage you to start thinking about home as an extended network, by acknowledging that you can (and sometimes must) get your emotional needs met in more than one place. Viewing your home as a stepping stone, rather than a millstone, is a subtle shift in mindset that keeps your energy focused on what you want to accomplish, rather than the ways in which your home might be holding you back. It's a concept we'll come back to in relation to some of the other emotional needs.

I'll leave you with an astute observation by Henry Ford, who said, 'Too many of us, when we accomplish what we set out to do, exclaim, "See what I have done!" instead of saying, "See where I have been led."' May your home lead you to all kinds of wonderful places.

5

Belonging

'There is something of yourself that you leave at every meeting with another person.'

Fred Rogers, Mister Rogers' Neighborhood

I've lived in Denmark for over a decade, but I still only speak what I jokingly refer to as 'Bakery Danish'. I can confidently order a wide selection of drinks and pastries in Copenhagen's finest eateries, deftly swallowing parts of whole words in a language that sounds like its native speakers are babbling away with hot porridge in their mouths. If it's a good day, I'll even manage to exchange a handful of pleasantries. But if the conversation takes a turn in any other direction, I'm adrift. It's a source of shame, my failure to learn the language, but English is so widely spoken that I can never bring myself to take the plunge. Even so, at least once a week I'll have some kind of encounter in which I'm at a literal loss for words and my status as a foreigner is plain to see. I'll feel terribly out of place, despite all the foundations of my life set out here. It makes me wonder: Is it ever possible to feel like you truly belong in a place when you do not share the most defining trait of its people, such as their language? What *does* it take to belong somewhere, and what do we experience when we feel 'out of place'?

Everyone I know and love has felt out of place at some point in their life. I'm quite certain you have, too. In research terms, this experience is best described as 'belonging uncertainty' – a term coined and explored by the social psychologist Geoffrey Cohen. This expression refers to the doubts we might have about our belongingness in any given situation, the effects of which can be devastating for our well-being. As Cohen says in his book *Belonging: The Science of Creating Connection and Bridging Divides*, 'When we perceive threats to our sense of belonging, our horizon of possibility shrinks.' This is certainly not limited to those who have moved abroad, seeing as any one of us can feel out of place and therefore at a remove from possibility, whether at school, work, in all kinds of social situations, and – yes – even in our own home.

A sense of belonging is about feeling you're accepted for who you are, by the people you live amongst and in spaces that reflect you. I like to say that belonging is knowing you're in the right place at the right time. The good news is that belonging has one of the smallest gaps between importance and reality at home, compared with other needs, but it still sits at 28 per cent overall, which suggests there are a lot of people living in ways that make them feel lonely, disconnected or misunderstood. When I look at this figure and all the insights behind it, I feel the implication clawing at my throat. Losing your sense of belonging can mimic grief, such a desperate feeling and totally unendurable. And like grief, the experience can make you feel at a loss for words to explain what's happening to you. Having access to the right kind of language to describe what you're feeling is a vital tool, particularly when that feeling is severely limiting how you live your life. Cohen's research on belonging shows that when new college students hear stories about the experiences of other students on their campus, their feelings of loneliness and belonging uncertainty are reduced. They understand they're not alone. The right words at the right time create meaning and connection. Simply talking about our need for belonging does half the job of creating it.

Thinking back to my dilemma of learning Danish, I believe the feeling of belonging *is* dependent on a kind of language, just not the kind you find in textbooks. The language of belonging is expressed through the in-jokes and shorthands, and all those shared reference points, values and memories that build bridges between all kinds of people. These elements are the *lingua franca* of connection and community, regardless of the fluency of the languages actually spoken.

If belonging is about being part of a community where communication is easy, like with a close friend or tight-knit group of colleagues, then it would make sense that this feeling frequently operates outside our immediate home, in other spaces and places. This often leads people to say that they *feel at home* when they get together with friends, family or community members with whom they share a profound sense of affinity. It's also heavily informed by our nationality or regionalism, and why so many of us feel like we belong in certain places, like particular cities or countries, even if we haven't been there for a long time. As a social species, we have evolved to gravitate towards being part of something bigger than us, whether that's a group of two people or a country of millions. Perhaps a sense of belonging explains why so many of us say we feel at home in two or more different places. If our feeling of accomplishment is enabled through the concept of the extended home, which I touched on at the end of the previous chapter, then it's only possible because we feel like we *belong* in those extended spaces and places. I think this is why people tend to shortcut the feeling of home as being a feeling of belonging.

When I ask people about belonging, many feel inclined to say that home is where their family is. I say 'inclined' because it feels a bit like received wisdom, rather than a lived reality. I've certainly lived in plenty of places with people I love where I still didn't feel at home. We need look no further than online expat groups to find people who relocated with their family because of their partner's job and are struggling to find their place. And what about the experiences of people who live alone? In the IKEA *Life at Home* research from 2022, we saw an uptick in people wanting to go solo, with as many as 13 per cent saying it's something they'd decided to do in the previous year. One woman we met said that living alone after her divorce was the first time she felt she belonged in her own home.

All this makes me think back to that lightbulb conversation with Professor Alison Blunt, when she described the sense of 'belonging personally and belonging collectively' as the core of home. It's clear that the feeling of belonging is a significant contributor to the feeling of home, and that it comes from much more than just living with your loved ones. To simplify this, I'd like to propose two defining characteristics of belonging which we'll focus on through my 'hands and heart' solutions:

- Belonging is powered by communication
- Belonging is an expression of identity

And to explain how, I'm going to take you from Copenhagen to New York City.

When I graduated from university, with my history degree taking pride of place on my extremely thin CV, I moved back home with my parents to have a textbook existential crisis in my childhood bedroom. I had no savings, no job offers and no idea. Sensing my desperation, my father gently suggested I pick up a few skills that would be more helpful than my ability to discuss the causes of the Franco-Prussian war. So, I'd get the bus into town on Tuesday afternoons to take a beginner's course in Microsoft Excel at the local college, learn a few keyboard shortcuts and cry on the ride home. A few weeks into this living nightmare, I got a temp job photocopying forms for the local health authority, whilst I continued to apply for increasingly unsuitable jobs in London. By lunchtime on my second shift, I had already hit my daily quota of photocopying and a colleague threw a phone at me because she thought I was trying to steal her job. I cried on the bus home that day, too, because her job was the very last thing I wanted.

That night, half a bottle of wine down, I sat on the end of my single bed and emptied my wallet. I had a dim recollection that I'd picked up one or two business cards during the Edinburgh Fringe, where I'd managed to swing a three-week internship, after graduating, with a guy who handled publicity for a cycling comedian. That was when I remembered Paul, with his peroxide-blonde hair, teddy-bear brown eyes and a laugh like a drain. He had given me his dog-eared card at a backstage party one night after we'd met and chatted about the handful of drag acts he was promoting. He said I could get in touch anytime. 'Anytime' felt good enough right about then.

If you're lucky, you'll meet a handful of people in your life who will change its course for the better. Paul changed mine the moment he replied to my email and agreed to let me come and work for him – and, it turned out, also crash at his place – for three months in New York City. I flew out two weeks later. As the plane banked above JFK Airport, I opened my wallet and for the hundredth time pulled out the piece of paper carrying the address Paul had given me. I tried to picture where I would be living, building a mental image from a composite of all the New York streetscapes and apartments I had seen in countless TV shows and films. There was a vague sense of familiarity, like remembering a dream hours after waking, as I watched the glittering roads and landmarks slowly rise beneath me, my nose pressed against the cabin window. The thing about living in New York, it turns out, is that it is exactly how you imagine it to be and nothing like you expect.

The urge to belong is a desire to feel part of a constellation. One of the first things I observed in Paul was how many times he'd eagerly say, 'There's someone I have to introduce you to.' This was how he moved through life, by connecting all the people he knew, one excitable introduction at a time. In seeking a constellation, Paul made it his mission to create galaxies. What I witnessed – and later evidenced through the IKEA research – is that when we feel we belong, we benefit from better health and well-being, better relationships and more optimism about our future. What I also saw was the important distinction between belonging and fitting in. As Brené Brown explained in *Atlas of the Heart*, 'Belonging is being accepted for being who you are. Fitting in is being accepted for being like everyone else.' Paul never fit in anywhere – he bucked every trend, from fashion to food – but he belonged amongst every single gathering or community he nurtured. He was the sun around which all our planets orbited.

I acquired a lifetime of wisdom about belonging in the few short months I spent in Paul's immediate company, and in the many years of friendship that followed. I want to share some simple but powerful 'hands and heart' ways to create more belonging in your own life at home, which I learned from this experience. These solutions meet our need to belong personally and collectively, and are substantiated by the findings from many years of *Life at Home* research. I believe they speak to a shared understanding of what can happen when we find ourselves in the right place at the right time.

Know your neighbours

The morning after I landed in New York, I headed downtown to meet Paul at his apartment. At that point, he was living on the third floor of a walk-up above a record shop on the Lower East Side, and as I waited for him to buzz me in, I soaked in the wild array of sounds and smells of this new environment. Paul came bounding down the stairs to greet me, and before we even dropped off my bag he took me to his neighbour's apartment so we could feed her pet goldfish, Fluffy, whilst she was away. Paul knew everyone on his block, regaling me with their comings and goings, their work and passions. 'You *have* to meet Erin – we'll go over later,' and on it went. It wasn't even 9 a.m.

A month later, I helped Paul move to an apartment in the heart of Hell's Kitchen which was part of a rent-controlled complex for people working in the arts and creative industries. He had been on the waiting list for eleven years, and before he'd even moved in, he already knew all of his neighbours. Paul could have one conversation with someone and that person would be in his orbit for life. It was intoxicating to witness, and made me feel ashamed of all the times I'd lived somewhere and couldn't even tell you my neighbours' names, let alone what their jobs or passions were.

One of the enduring lessons of the Covid-19 lockdown was the important role of our neighbourhoods in our mental health and well-being. When we couldn't see friends and family who lived far away, we became deeply reliant on a sense of belonging with those we lived amongst. In fact, during the 2021 IKEA research 73 per cent of people said they'd spent more time in their neighbourhoods in the preceding twelve months, and 62 per cent said their health and well-being had improved as a result of this sense of neighbourly belonging. Paul didn't need a pandemic to tell him this. He instinctively knew that connections between neighbours establish two important things:

- **The safety from an immediate support network that holds everyone together**
  Our ability to survive and thrive is intrinsic to being a social species.
- **The exponential energy that occurs when people have the opportunity to connect frequently**
  We can do, be and dream bigger and better when we create abundant social energy, like bumping into neighbours every day.

Figures from the US-based Pew Research Center before the pandemic revealed the general state of affairs in America, where 57 per cent of people said they knew only some of their neighbours and a quarter of people aged under thirty said they didn't know *any* of their neighbours. Various lockdowns may have unleashed the potential for deeper neighbourly affection for a brief moment, but the *Life at Home* research indicates that this feeling has ebbed away in the subsequent years, as restrictions lifted, and we continue to follow the trend of fewer and fewer of us knowing who our neighbours are – let alone hanging out with them. This is a problem, given the clear well-being benefits we saw when people spent more time with the people on their doorstep. As recently as 2023, one in five people felt a sense of belonging from having shared values with others in their community, and one in four people who live alone said they get a sense of belonging by chatting with a neighbour.

This is why my first solution to building a sense of belonging at home is to **get to know your neighbours**. You don't have to be best mates who are deeply in the pockets of each other's lives, but the relationships should centre on two things:

- Regular conversation
- Mutual kindness and support

No matter whether you live in an inner-city apartment or a detached house in a sparsely populated village, make a point of smiling at your closest neighbours and saying hello every day. If you have quite literally never done this before, despite living next door to them for years, it might feel jarring to suddenly shift your focus in their direction. Here are some tried-and-tested opportunities that lend themselves to nurturing better neighbourly relations:

- → **When neighbours move in**
  Fresh slate! No one will think you've had a personality transplant if you knock on the door and offer a helping hand or a small pot plant as a housewarming gift. This is the best opportunity to establish ongoing conversation and the offer of help when they need it.

- → **When people have a baby**
  I can attest to the fact that every new parent will be delighted to know that you are on hand if things get overwhelming, and that you are super-chill about the fact that babies are notorious for disturbing the peace. I've used these opportunities to drop off baked goodies and hot meals to various exhausted and weepy parents, along with our phone numbers and an emphatic reminder that they can get in touch *whenever*. You do not need to be a parent to show up for neighbours with new arrivals.

→ **When you have a DIY project on the go**
As a matter of courtesy, it's nice to let your neighbours know if you're going to be banging, drilling or sanding your way through the evenings and weekends. Good manners aside, if you need a certain kind of tool or level of expertise, consider your neighbours your first port of call before you fork out cash hiring gear or professionals. You'd be amazed at the kind of equipment people have lurking in their lock-ups and garages. When I was refurbishing my hallway cupboard, I borrowed my neighbour's professional-grade electric drill (swiftly followed by his ability to wield it safely), which meant I also got a few tips on how to tackle future DIY projects.

→ **When there's a reason to celebrate**
Christmas, Hanukkah, Eid, summer solstice, Halloween . . . Whatever your religion, practice, culture or tradition, if it's important to you, why not share the celebrations with your neighbours? For the last five years, I've baked Christmas cookies for everyone in our apartment block. It takes me a few hours to pull together thirteen gift bags of biscuits, but I sing along to Christmas tunes and now my daughter helps me decorate and deliver them, so it's become part of our family tradition, too.

Other simple but creative ideas I've seen from various home research visits over the years include starting a communal stairwell library, sharing freshly cut flowers or a surplus of herbs and veggies from your garden, and establishing a neighbourhood flea market or clothes swap. Extending effort and support to others makes it easier to solicit things in return when you need them. My neighbours have gladly helped us out in some needy situations, like feeding our cat for a week when I was hospitalized during labour. One memorable Christmas Eve a neighbour gladly gave me a packet of cloves when I realized, after the shops had shut, that these were missing for a very specific Danish recipe. Maybe it was the festive spirit(s), but that particular act of kindness made me quite weepy.

People will come and go during your time in any home, and connections will be lost, but if you are intentional about maintaining a regular rhythm of conversation, and mutual kindness and support, there'll always be a beating heart of belonging amongst your neighbours.

We belong together

Paul had lived alone for years before I rolled out my sleeping bag for a season. I'd always had the impression that it would take some kind of divine intervention for him to consider leaving his rent-controlled single digs behind, so it was all the more special when he eventually met the man who would become his husband, and they became utterly inseparable whilst continuing to enjoy their own homes.

Even though the emotional gap for belonging is at the smaller end, relative to the other seven emotional needs of the home, it still presents a sizeable problem. It seems odd that we would willingly live with people with whom we do not feel acceptance and affinity, yet many of us do, though we struggle to explain it. For those of you who dwell with disconnection, it may be because you have no choice about who shares your living quarters, like students or retirees in co-living arrangements; or maybe we live with people we're related to but they're unaccepting of our values or self-expression, or simply not curious about who we are. More often than not, we live with people we love dearly but we're just so goddam busy that we de-prioritize connection.

Most people assume that if you live with family – especially a family you've created with someone else – then you get a side order of belonging ready-made with the deal. I often think about the young woman in Japan who told us during a home research visit that the only place in her home where she feels she belongs is the bathroom. In the bedroom she's a wife, in the kitchen she's a cook, in the living room she's a mother, at her computer she's a colleague ... But in the bathroom she can fully be herself. I guess that if you start to feel like a pie, with slices handed out to those around you, depending on their tastes and needs, it's harder to show up as the whole of yourself. This might explain why the *Life at Home* research has shown, over the years, that parents living with their young families say they experience a lack of belonging at home *more* than people of other ages and in different situations.

You don't have to be raising a family to know what it's like to have your life allocated across many different relational roles, given that all of us have experience of being a friend, a partner or a colleague, to name just a few. What's for certain is that a marriage certificate or shared DNA doesn't implicitly create belonging at home. The rise of the Chosen Family is a good rejoinder to the popular saying that 'blood is thicker than water', especially for people whose identities are not respected by their origin families. It's also important to remember that love and belonging are not the same thing. You can love someone you live with deeply, but struggle to know how to connect with them or show up as your whole self.

This is important context for the simple but effective solutions I'm proposing, because they're designed to help you create a greater sense of belonging with the people you live with, no matter if that's your partner and kids or the new flatmate who replied to the advert for your spare room. However, these approaches will struggle to scratch the surface if other important things are amiss. Some relationships suffer from a profound lack of communication – and, in some instances, respect – to the extent that there's much deeper work that needs to be done before you can start layering in the kinds of actions I suggest. If you find yourself here, then seeking the help of a trained professional, like a therapist, might be the best course of action for you over the longer term.

If you're still with me by this point, then you'll be delighted to know that we've come to the part of the book where I finally introduce *hygge* to proceedings. If you live outside Denmark, you probably think *hygge* is a design aesthetic focused on scented candles and cashmere throws. If so, you might be surprised to learn that *hygge* is both a noun and a verb, which is an efficient way to position a concept which is otherwise almost untranslatable. It's precisely this effect of being both a description and an action which places *hygge* firmly in the context of belonging. The Danes will ask, '*Skal vi hygge*?', which essentially means 'Shall we get together and create a welcoming environment where we can relax, have fun, connect and make cosy memories?' See? Totally untranslatable. All you need to remember is that when you *hygge* with people, you feel like you belong.

So, here are a handful of highly effective *hygge* highlights to cultivate belonging with the people you live with. Of course, you are more than welcome to light a few scented candles when you give them a go.

> → **Make time for people**
> Time is the most valuable gift you can bestow on someone you love. Full stop. Making time for someone in an otherwise busy and multi-purpose home says you're committed to the relationship and care deeply about that person. What you do

with that time is up to you and the passions and preferences of the person involved, but it should be free from distractions (put your phone away, put the kids to bed, use a quiet part of the home, etc.) and easy to commit to. There's something quite heartbreaking about a consistently broken promise of time spent together because something 'more important' cropped up.

→ **Get curious**
Belonging is an expression of identity. It's entirely possible to live with someone and never truly know them, so the best way to establish better belonging is to understand who they are. It's no harder than asking open-ended questions that show you're curious about what makes them tick — and making eye contact whilst you do it; it deeply reinforces verbal connections and lets people know they've been seen.

→ **Praise and appreciate**
We seem to think that feedback and praise are only for the workplace, but showing appreciation for someone is important in the home, too. We get so used to everyone performing the domestic or familial roles they're assigned, we simply come to expect that dinner will be served, clothes will be laundered, the trash taken out and the Lego tidied up. Take a moment to

thank the person who cooked the meal, or let someone know that you like the flowers they picked. We're more likely to experience belonging when we know we're making a contribution that's valued, but often the only way we know that is if someone tells us.

→ **Show who you are**
When you look around your home, does it feel like everyone lives there? What I mean is, do the contents and interior designs of your space speak to everyone's presence and identity? Or is it all about one, single approach? Seeing ourselves reflected in the space around us means we're far more likely to view our home in a positive way, compared with those who feel their home doesn't show who they are. I talk a lot more about identity in the next chapter, but there is something simple you can do at this stage to ensure better representation at home: ask everyone to make at least one choice about the look and feel of the space. This could range from a single object to the colour of the walls. If this feels hard for some people, suggest they choose a new house plant – as I discussed in Chapter 2, plants are a great entry point for feeling more in control of the space around you.

The great thing about *hygge* is that it works with people across your life, no matter your relationships with them. Investing time, curiosity, appreciation and personalization will help ensure that the people you live with will have the *hygge*-iest experience of all.

Invite people in

If you've spent any time in New York City, you'll know it's a place where people go out more than they stay in. Minuscule kitchens and an abundance of affordable and delicious dining options on the doorstep make eating out an inevitability. So, Paul and I dined out a lot, way more than I ever had before, but Paul still entertained at home whenever he could, despite living in what amounted to a two-room apartment the size of a camper van. Paul owned one chair and a repurposed church pew, so meals were served family-style from big sharing platters whilst we all sat cross-legged on his Moroccan rug. But what he lacked in space and culinary flair (braised sprouts were his go-to), he more than made up for with a heavy-handed pour and wicked sense of humour. I didn't know about *hygge* back then, but it was clearly dialled up to 11.

Those evenings created pathways to people I'd have most likely never otherwise met. It's quite something to pass the sprouts to long-term AIDS survivors, drag kings and queens, playwrights, journalists, philanthropists and activists, especially if you were plugging data into Excel spreadsheets and crying on the bus the week before. It had this telescoping effect which meant that whenever I met up with Paul in the years that followed, he'd often invite me to parties and dinners that other people were hosting because I'd met so-and-so before, *remember?* By the time I left, it felt like I'd shared a plate of hummus and a bottle of red wine with half of New York.

Whilst our opportunity to connect with people often plays out in many different places where we might find and spend time with like-minded people, from a place of worship to online gaming forums (or the various eateries of the Big Apple), there's something potent about bringing people together at home. Paul had clearly observed the kinetic energy that comes from hosting in your most familiar of spaces. He wasn't just inviting people into his home, he was inviting them into his life. Data from the IKEA *Life at Home* Report 2023 showed that a third of us believe that laughing with friends is one of the best things about being together, and whilst laughter is spontaneous and cannot be directed (*laugh, goddammit!*), it responds gorgeously to a few primers in a space where we can control our privacy and comfort. Namely, the home. For any of this to happen, we must invite people in.

I love going over to other people's homes. Mainly it's because, thanks to my work, I'm obsessed with knowing more about the different ways people live. But I find you can only really get to know someone properly when you step inside their world. To bring someone new into your home is an expression of intimacy and vulnerability, like lifting the lid and letting someone see how it works inside. That's why it's so important to reciprocate, to open yourself up and find that common ground. On countless occasions, I've visited a friend at home only to discover that they paint, throw clay, collect memorabilia, or – and this is true – play the didgeridoo, months or even years into meeting them. In his book *Blink*, which is about the science of gut decisions, Malcolm Gladwell shares a remarkable piece of research led by the psychologist Samuel Gosling which looked into intuitive judgement processes. In one particular study, as Gladwell recounts it, Gosling asked strangers to spend no more than fifteen minutes in a number of student dorm rooms, then answer some questions about each of the students' personalities based on what they had seen in their bedroom. The strangers were significantly more accurate at predicting three of the Big Five personality traits amongst the students, including conscientiousness and openness to new experiences, than actual friends of the students were. This was all from a quick eyeball around their room. As Gladwell writes, 'you can learn as much – or more – from one glance at a private space as you can from hours of exposure to a public face'.

If you've found yourself taking a peek at people's possessions and snooping through their storage when you've been invited over, you're definitely not alone. One in twenty people admitted as much when asked about it for the IKEA *Life at Home* Report 2023. I'm honestly surprised it's not higher. Rest assured, I'm not busy rifling through medicine cabinets and underwear drawers with a clipboard when I visit friends, but I do find that the opportunity to see how people curate their personal spaces – both intentionally and inadvertently – gives me a deeper insight into who they are and what makes them tick than when we get together outside of home. I tend to walk away full of happiness and feeling deeply inspired – by their approach to interior design, by their skills in the kitchen or by seeing the things that honour their passions and accomplishments. No wonder that one in five people globally say they're most inspired by the homes of their friends when they consider making changes to their own home, and this response is particularly prevalent amongst younger people. From where I'm standing, unless you have a secret family living under your stairs, there's almost nothing that would threaten our relationship if you invited me into your home. All it ever does is grow empathy and understanding, and deepen our connection.

However, extending an invitation to friends, old or new, can feel challenging if you're not in the habit of doing it. The fear of rejection can stop us from even trying. Also – oh God – the *effort* of hosting. Who has the time to clean, cook and coordinate? And then there's the anxiety about what you're actually going to *do* together and if everyone's going to get along. It's just easier to go out, right? You can see how easy it is to talk yourself out of nurturing connection and belonging in your own home – even when you know it's good for you – and outsource it to other people and places.

If the proposition of hosting feels like it comes

loaded with a groaning list of to-do's, then I'd like to start by telling you what you do *not* have to do. A list of to-*don'ts*, if you like:

> → **You do not have to clean your home from top to bottom**
> No one is going to look for dust behind the radiator, I promise.
>
> → **You do not have to pretend your kids have moved out**
> Toys, clutter, clothes . . . It's totally normal for your home to look like its occupants live there.
>
> → **You do not have to serve a three-course meal for twelve people**
> You are not a restaurant. You don't even have to cook.
>
> → **You do not need to get dressed up**
> Lint-roller the pet hair off your clothes if you want, but it's not essential.
>
> → **You do not have to apologize for the lack of space, seats, unchipped crockery, and so on**
> Again, these are apologies for just living in your home.

Now that the ground rules are in place, let's consider what you *could* do when you ask people to come over:

- **Keep it small and simple**
  Start by inviting over your closest friend or a family member. If you're totally new to a place and in the process of finding your people, invite a neighbour over. Make some coffee, open a packet of biscuits and ask them how their day is going. That's literally all you need to do.

- **Decide on one activity to take the pressure off you to constantly entertain**
  Movie evenings are lovely, or a good-natured games night with some classics like *Cluedo* or *Scrabble*. If you have a hobby you'd like to share, invite people over to form a book club or a knitting circle, for example.

- **Ask everyone to bring a dish**
  Make it a themed potluck, or split the courses amongst your guests so they bring nibbles, a starter and dessert. Then you can just focus on preparing one thing.

- **Be clear about when it ends**
  This is particularly helpful when it involves children with boundless energy or parties that seem to go on for ever. Letting people know when you intend to escort them to the door before they've even set foot in your home might seem a little impertinent, but the reality is

> that everyone has a better time when they know they're not overstaying their welcome and you don't have to look pointedly at your watch.

In truth, there's only one thing you have to do to invite people into your home, and that's to invite them. We're a social species and we've been sitting around a fire back at someone's cave since the dawn of time, so why stop now?

Your home doesn't need a uniform

If you've spent any time on social media, you'd be forgiven for thinking that everyone but you is doing some kind of home renovation. You'd also be forgiven for thinking that they're all renovating the *same* home, such is the ubiquity of their choice of colour, style and approach. I talked a lot about the tyranny of comparison – a thief of comfort – in Chapter 1, but I want to revisit it here in the context of belonging.

If you take a bird's eye view of the major global shifts which have occurred over the last decade, you'll see an increase in social fragmentation. This is more than likely to continue as we witness more of the fabric that binds communities weaken under the pressure of persistent inequality. One of the most egregious impacts of this problem is the ever-growing distance between 'the haves' and 'the have-nots' in terms of global resources, access and opportunities. And obviously this is heavily intersected by ethnicity, gender, sexuality and other identity markers.

This is, to put it lightly, some pretty heavy stuff to be wrapping our heads around as we ponder what creates the feeling of home. So, why am I raising it now? Well, social fragmentation strips away the broad commonalities between people and starts to place certain requirements on which your participation in various groups rests. These requirements might ask you to change things about yourself and your home which are not true to your authentic self, yet you feel pressure to conform, because being on the outside of the group is social exile and humans are *wired* for connection. We start to blur the lines between what we have and who we are.

When I helped Paul move into his new apartment in Hell's Kitchen, I spent the best part of a week gently packing his enormous collection of *tchotchkes*. It's a Yiddish word long used by Jewish-Americans to describe trinkets or bric-a-brac. Paul was not Jewish, but he loved the way the word felt in his mouth. Trinkets are cheap, but *tchotchkes* are for life. Before we moved his belongings over, Paul walked me through his new home, proudly explaining where his two-metre-long bespoke desk, made from a salvaged piece of driftwood, was going to go, and pointing out the wall for the ornate Murphy bed he was getting from an obscure shop on the Upper West Side. He had no more than 40 square metres of space to play with – it was one-and-a-half rooms, at best – but you'd think he had the whole of Las Vegas's Bellagio Hotel at his disposal, such was his excitement about how much he could do with so little.

Once the last of the *tchotchkes* had been unpacked – a golden pig, positioned in his bathroom – we cracked open a bottle of wine to celebrate and listened to someone practising the trumpet down the hall. By that point I was staying on an inflatable mattress on his floor, the both of us living out of our suitcases until he found the right kind of closet and I took my return flight home. Looking around his apartment, I realized I had no idea where Paul got his interior-design inspiration. The ideas just seemed to bubble up within him, fully formed. Paul brought things into his home for the simple reason that he *really liked them,* no matter whether they matched anything else. His home already felt so full and lived-in, so utterly *his*.

When the invitations from his neighbours came thick and fast over the following days, I realized that no two apartments were anything alike. Even if the footprint was the same, the layouts, styles and colourways were all wildly different. We'd have coffee with 18A amongst their gilt-edged mock Regency seating and a sea of flamboyant damask fabrics, followed by cocktails with 32E in a haze of burnt umber walls and stripped wooden chairs. Where else could any of these individuals possibly belong but together under one enormous roof? There were no 'haves' and 'have-nots' in this particular slice of New York real estate, and no identity marker for living there other than showing up as yourself.

That's why my last solution is a simple proposition:

> **You have a choice** – to find out where you belong, or work out how to fit in. To which of the two will you give your precious time and energy?

If you need a nudge, I can assure you that if you spend your whole life trying to fit in, you will be miserable. I've spent the best part of this chapter encouraging you to open up your life at home, create connection and communication, and to invite people in. This is contingent on you bringing your true self to the table. Again, belonging is an expression of identity. You will never belong anywhere if you never show up as yourself. If you keep saying you'll have people over just as soon as you've redone the kitchen or sorted out the clutter in the living room or moved somewhere bigger, then you're putting all your energy into fitting in. Your home doesn't need to wear a uniform for you to belong.

Paul and I stayed firm friends over the years, seeing each other as much as distance would allow. Whenever I returned to New York, just banking over JFK triggered a feeling of home; the sense that I belonged in this extraordinary city because Paul was down there somewhere. Every time we met, he'd invite me and whoever I was with to a party, dinner or recital, nearly always taking place at one of his friends' houses. I'd probably once met them over braised sprouts, but even if I hadn't, he nurtured this expansive generosity of friendship and belonging amongst everyone he knew. They always welcomed me in.

A few months after I moved to Denmark, I went to a talk hosted by an English-language magazine on the topic of what it means to be an immigrant in Copenhagen. I heard from two activist creatives and sisters, Seda and Şeyda Özçetin, who moved to Copenhagen from Turkey with their mother in 2011. Their experience is a complex story of what it takes to stay in a place you have come to call home, to be derailed by politics and sickness, but they put their finger on something shared by people whose lives are forged by living in many different places. I have no claim on New York beyond a clutch of months living there, but I feel its presence almost every day in the way I show up in the world. Rather than give a granular account of their own migration journey, the Özçetin sisters had simply started telling people that they '*feel* from Copenhagen'. They even sold T-shirts bearing this slogan. I also feel from Copenhagen. And I feel from New York, too. What I feel is a sense of belonging – that I am in the right place at the right time.

The last time I saw Paul was at a rooftop party on the Upper East Side. We drank cocktails and spat olive stones over the side – a long-standing ritual initiated by his friend Betsy, who liked to kick-start Martini Season this way. I chatted with Paul's husband, Kendall, about our mutual love of the late Danish architect Finn Juhl and we made excitable plans for them both to come and stay with me sometime so we could all visit Finn Juhl's glorious house just north of Copenhagen. Several drinks down, we went for dinner at a classic neighbourhood Italian joint and ate huge bowls of spaghetti and meatballs by candlelight. By the time I left for my hotel, rain was pouring down and the taxi lights and street lamps were casting a kaleidoscopic sheen on the wet ground. We ran down the road, laughing and hooting as we kicked up the puddles. A quick squeeze goodbye, with promises to meet again soon. *Not so long until the next time.*

Some of our final messages passed between us less than a year later, when, on different sides of the ocean, we both suddenly found ourselves in hospital – me in premature labour, he with terminal brain cancer. I've not been back to New York since Paul passed away. Part of me is afraid to find out what it will feel like to be in that city and not have him there. Will it still feel like home? In *The Colossus of New York*, the writer Colson Whitehead provides an extraordinary account of what it means to live in New York and then leave it one day. He writes about the sense-memory of a place so preserved in our hearts that we cannot fathom it changing once we are gone: 'Maybe we become New Yorkers the day we realize that New York will go on without us.' This is what belonging asks of you when it reaches into the extended home to multiple places and spaces – you must make peace with the fact that you can't fix it in time or preserve it in aspic. It's a tough pill, but I'd rather know belonging and then lose it, than never know it at all.

The best way to honour the people we have loved and lost – those with whom we felt we belonged – is to continue their work. Paul ultimately knew that creating community and connection is an act of service.

That's why he always asked anyone he met, 'How can I help you?' That's why he replied to my email all those years ago. Belonging thrives on inclusive communication, and it withers when we hold ourselves back, make our voices small and our actions even smaller. I hope this chapter inspires you to create your own constellation of belonging, by getting to know your neighbours, deepening your connections with those at home and inviting people in. I also hope it helps you understand the tension between belonging and fitting in, which so many of us find ourselves caught between. Above all, I hope this chapter guides you to the kind of belonging which is born through service to those around you.

If you don't know what to do, take a leaf out of Paul's book and try asking this: *'How can I help you?'* It's a question that can't help but spark the kind of connections that become entire constellations.

6

Nurturing

'Seek home for rest, for home is best.'

> Thomas Tusser, *Five Hundred Points of*
> *Good Husbandry (1573)*

WHEN WE WERE EXPLORING THE feeling of belonging together, in the previous chapter, I asked you a question: Does your home reflect your identity? If you didn't think about it then, take a moment to do so now.

When we've asked that question through IKEA's *Life at Home* research, we've found that around four in ten people globally didn't feel their home was a reflection of themselves. When we've dug deeper, we've found that the most important identity markers for people at home are the things they own – especially pieces they've bought for themselves or inherited – followed by the space to do the things they love, then the people they live with. I've lived in plenty of places where I've had no say over the furniture, wall colour or room allocation – and, in several instances, the people living with me – and I've almost always found a reason to spend time away. Homes that don't feel like 'us' are instinctively off-putting. It's like being stuck next to someone at a dinner party with whom you have nothing in common. We wouldn't maintain a friendship (let alone a relationship) with someone who doesn't see us for who we are, so why would we put up with living in a home that does the same?

Whilst all the eight emotional needs have interdependencies, I've often felt that belonging and nurturing are most closely connected. What unites them is the role of identity:

* When we seek belonging, we're hoping to find ourselves in relation to other people and places
* When we seek nurturing, we're hoping to find ourselves within

When we nurture ourselves, we're extending a kindness and an invitation inwards. We're attending to ourselves. It's an opportunity to get in touch with who we are and make amends to our well-being. I see a virtuous feedback loop between self-expression and self-care, whereby the practice of self-care gives us the chance to connect with the deepest part of ourselves, and when we're comfortable with the authenticity we find there, we can open ourselves up to experience the breadth of well-being benefits.

If we're good at nurturing, it means we're consistently reaching for certain actions that we know will make us feel better in body and mind because we understand who we are and what makes us tick. They're routines but with a higher purpose. Perhaps an easier way to talk about nurturing actions is to call them rituals. By practising these rituals, we deftly bring together the identity markers of objects, spaces and people. This is why home is a great space for nurturing, because we're in easy reach of these three components and we can also establish boundaries around them. Home is also typically a space where we have cultivated comfort, control and security – and when these emotional needs are in place, it's far easier to go deeper with our other ones.

Nowadays, when we talk about self-care and self-expression, people can get a bit eye-roll-y. It's as if the idea of taking care of ourselves has become associated with weakness, and we're all too soft for the hard slog of life. It seems that hustle culture wants us to sprint through life until we hit a wall, and only then, under the banner of 'breakdown' or 'burnout', are we entitled to access the full range of responses which will aid our recovery. When I was running towards my own wall a few years ago, I read *Wintering* by Katherine May. It's a beautiful book exploring the ways we can embrace difficult changes in our life and unleash the power of rest and retreat. As May says, 'Doing those deeply unfashionable things – slowing down, letting your spare time expand, getting enough sleep, resting – is a radical act now, but it is essential.' When we asked what the number one priority is for an ideal home in the *Life at Home* research in 2023, overall, people said the ability to unwind and relax. Tellingly, however, this was considered far more important amongst older people, such as baby-boomers, than it was for Gen Z. It's almost as if the minute your parents have anything to do with something, you just don't want to touch it.

These deeply unfashionable things are the cornerstones of many rituals but we can't always see the value they hold, like unpolished gems. Going back a bit, when we explored the topic of well-being in the *Life at Home* research in 2021, we found that people said that sleeping and relaxing were the two most important activities for their mental well-being, which seemed obvious. But the biggest revelation was that when people treated these two actions as rituals, *it made them more effective*. This is a great insight to start with, as we explore nurturing, because you almost certainly have a lot of those unpolished gems at home already.

I want to home in on the way that rituals allow us to self-care and self-express. At this point, you might feel a bit unsure about what a ritual actually is, especially when it's applied to things you probably already do without thinking, like having dinner or going to bed. You might even be at a loss to describe *any* rituals you perform at home. I have a remarkably simple test that will immediately make apparent any rituals you have which are hiding in plain sight: go and stay in someone else's home.

Until the meteoric rise of Airbnb, it wasn't typical to spend much time in the homes of people you didn't know. Now there are more than 4 million people acting as 'hosts' to upward of 1.4 billion guests around the world. I expect you've been one of them. Anyone who's stayed in an Airbnb has some kind of insane story – our first visit to Copenhagen culminated in an aborted drug deal (not ours) and our host's friend (ostensibly there just to hand over the key) fleeing from the apartment in his underpants. But most of the time, it's *fine*. The sheets are clean, the fridge works, and there are some decent reads on the bookshelf. It's just never usually to your taste. It's a strange sensation, to cos-play as people you've never met in their own home. It immediately makes clear the power of self-expression, because we always feel a bit wrongfooted by the interior design choices other people make that run contrary to ours. *Who chooses to live like this?* I'll find myself muttering as I remove the anchor from their nautically themed bathroom and put their crystal pig collection out of the reach of my children.

But the thing I struggle with most when I stay in an Airbnb is how much harder it is to maintain my self-care rituals. Many of the things I do to express and nurture myself are reliant on simple tools, like having a bedside light so I can read before I go to sleep, or a bathroom mirror at the right height so I can slather various lotions on my face. I know it's got bad when I stop journaling every day because they don't have a desk and I forgot to bring the lovely little fountain pen my husband bought me. Who is this person, writing about her life with a *Biro* on the *sofa*? Even if we can cobble together the things we need to read and write, or kick back with a face mask on, it uses so much more mental energy working out how to do it in a home that isn't ours. When we have to consciously think about it, the action moves from being habitual and automatic to specific and considered. As I discussed in Chapter 4, it is much harder to accomplish things at home when they're not part of a habituated routine. When this happens to me, I feel myself slackening, as though the threads of my identity are unravelling. Living somewhere that doesn't support your care is tolerable only for as long as the duration of the stay, but not a minute more. So, what happens if your own home makes you feel that way?

In my twenties, moving fearlessly through jobs, I lived in all four compass points of London. Having been born in a hospital on Highgate Hill, I tribally felt myself to be a North Londoner, but for many years I lived east of the city, in the borough of Bow. Here I reconnected with an old university friend, Isabella, who had come back from a stint in China, and we moved in together in a new-build flat her mother had just bought. Isabella and I had lived together before, just for a summer between academic years whilst we were studying in Edinburgh. It seemed a reasonable-enough trial basis to approach a more permanent arrangement. I was delighted.

I suspect, now, that most of that summer we first lived together was spent out of the house, where we'd been enjoying the good weather and the many delights of the Edinburgh Festival. The reality was that, under normal proceedings, we approached our domestic lives with such jarring difference that we gave each other whiplash. I was a one-woman cyclone, leaving behind strewn clothes, books, make-up, food, dirty dishes, with scalding hair-straighteners burning a hole in the carpet in my wake. Isabella was fastidiously tidy and exceedingly well put-together, and she watched my chaos from an increasingly weary distance. In a neutral environment, perhaps we could have found our way to domestic bliss. But with Isabella's mother as our landlord, the power dynamic was always going to be a little off. Nothing was ever intentionally said or done that made me feel like it wasn't my home – they were both endlessly kind and gracious – but the odds were always stacked against me. As we know from Chapter 2, homeowners are more likely than renters to say they feel in control of how their home is organized and how it looks, and feeling in control of our home makes it easier to personalize, so we feel reflected by the space around us. This is a trajectory that gets better with age, as over time we're more likely to accumulate things that reflect our personality. I had nothing to bring to the table.

In hindsight, I must have been a complete mess to live with. I was making my way through a chain of bad break-ups, overworking and partying too hard. I was trying to find myself after moving countries, jobs and home a hell of a lot. I found that harder in an environment where the custom was to clean up the kitchen before I sat down to eat (which was wildly at odds with my upbringing), and I had no emotional connection to the gorgeous Asian silk textiles hanging on the walls. So, I probably acted out a bit, pushing my self-expression into spaces outside of the flat whenever I ran into problems at home. Isabella snapped one day over something small that finally tipped her over the edge – crumbs on the kitchen floor, I recall – and we argued and cried and talked and laughed until we sank to the floor of the hallway between our bedrooms and held hands. As the great Dolly Parton once said, 'You can't make old friends.' Isabella and I shared a history which held some important fragments of my identity, and that was worth holding on to.

With technicolour twenty-twenty vision thanks to my research goggles, I can now see the problem for what it really was. When I went home every day, I couldn't find myself inside. This was partly because the space around me felt quite disconnected from my own taste, style and identity markers, and partly because I didn't know how to nurture myself in that environment. There was nothing bad or wrong about that home – it was clean and comfortable and secure, and Isabella and I had a good laugh when I wasn't accidentally squirting pomegranate juice on the white kitchen walls. It just wasn't *me*. If you had asked me to describe myself back then, as a twenty-something urbanite, I almost certainly would have reached for words that were action-orientated, like 'ambitious' and 'productive' and 'smart'. I'm not sure I'd even taken stock of what my values were, or what motivated me deep inside, beyond metrics like money and promotions. It didn't sit easy. When I was alone, at home, I started to feel the disconnect between the person who slayed at work on four hours' sleep and the person who deeply needed to rest and recentre themselves, with nowhere to go. My biggest problem was that I had routines that got me through twenty-four relentless hours on any given day, but I lacked rituals that were going to get me through life.

What is the alchemy that transforms a routine into a ritual, and why does that transformation create more impact in our life? Looking back at my own experiences, and hearing from peers at this stage of my life who are mostly stretched thin with responsibilities, I wonder if the value we glean from rituals has to do with how we value ourselves. Do we believe we are worthy of the time and energy we must extend in nurturing acts? Perhaps self-care can read as selfish, and we're afraid of looking like we're taking away from others when we give to ourselves. Or perhaps we still don't know ourselves well enough – or even *like* ourselves enough – to hold our value in a safe space. Certainly, self-care and self-worth operate on the same principle – that we are prepared and willing to stand up for ourselves.

If I pinpoint when things changed for me and I started welcoming nurturing into my life, it was on the heels of a scaldingly bad break-up. This cleaving forced me to reckon with who I was when I was on my own. Whilst I spent that first night as a singleton sobbing with a friend, I realized that one of the most frightening prospects ahead of me was what I was going to do with all my free time. I'll spare you the gory details of quite how much of a state I was in and for how long, and simply say that I finally turned a corner when I asked myself two questions that would go on to frame everything that followed in my life afterwards:

- Am I in touch with myself?
- Am I being kind to myself?

Nowadays, these two questions form the spine of the nurturing practices I conduct in my daily life. If I can answer them in the affirmative, I know that I am standing up for myself. If the answer is no, then it's clear that I need more opportunities for self-expression and self-care. These opportunities are built around a simple approach to developing rituals at home using my 'hands and heart' solutions. The great news is that these solutions intersect with some of the other solutions I've already mapped out across our other emotional needs, so if you're struggling to place rituals in your domestic life, I'm really confident we can crack this together.

As a rule, nurturing rituals have three parts:

> ❋ **A clear purpose**
> Why is this particular routine important? What's the intention?
>
> ❋ **A series of enabling behaviours**
> What do I need to do? How do I need to show up?
>
> ❋ **The right environment and boundaries**
> What are the contextual elements to my rituals?

Let's take a look at how this works in practical terms, when it comes to life at home.

Start with why

Newly single and wrung out of tears, I contemplated that first weekend without any couple-y plans with something akin to dread. That was when I decided that I would take myself out for a date. And not just any old date – I wanted to properly *woo* myself. Throw everything at it, like it was the love of a lifetime. This simple proposition of doing things with myself was initially about finding an excuse for being alone, which I otherwise viewed with horror, but it had the unintended consequence of revealing who I actually was. Turns out that when you make all the decisions about what to do with yourself, you only do the things you want to do. It whittles away all the crap you've been doing in service of other people.

I thoroughly recommend taking yourself on a date. It's a way of exploring what you like to do and how you want to behave when you stop maintaining appearances for other people. What it actually does is help you get in touch with the most authentic part of your motivations, and that gets you closer to your 'why'. Asking why we do the things we do isn't an existential question – it's a practical one. Asking 'why' is how we differentiate between a habituated routine and the meaningful practice of a ritual.

I'm going to combine a few of the 'hands and heart' solutions we worked through in previous chapters which are fantastic building blocks for getting to your 'why' when it comes to establishing rituals at home. When we explored **control**, we took the opportunity to ask better questions of ourselves. This kind of curiosity is an important quality to carry through to nurturing. When we explored **security**, in the context of privacy, I asked you to consider what you would do if you suddenly had one hour of time alone. All of these actions will tend to your needs in some way or another. And when we explored **accomplishment**, I wanted you to reflect on where you saw yourself a year from now. This 'big picture' thinking is how we get in touch with our motivations.

So, let's bring this all together:

> → **I want you to imagine you have twenty-four hours to yourself at home** – no people, responsibilities or obligations to deal with. All the people you love and care for are safe and happy, and there will be no crises or chores to divert your attention. You are allowed – no, you are *required* – to spend this time entirely in service to yourself. What will you do? Write it down.

I took the liberty of doing this exercise after a particularly challenging week spent juggling competing demands and a lot of Big Feelings, which meant that the thought of twenty-four hours to myself actually made me moan with longing. Once I'd jotted it all down, it became immediately apparent that I was using quite a lot of this theoretical time to catch up on life admin, like sorting out my kids' chest of drawers. The tendency to crack through a to-do list speaks volumes about where we place self-care in the hierarchy of values, which is to say it's somewhere at the bottom once we've bleached the toilet and filed our tax return. You might even feel that you cannot relax enough to do something good and kind for yourself *until* you've bleached the toilet and filed your tax return. That sentiment came through a fair amount in the *Life at Home* research from 2023, where people talked about the completion of domestic chores as an essential part of how they relax and unwind. There's a small addendum to this exercise – the actions you choose cannot be 'one and done', but things that you would enjoy doing repeatedly, over the course of a day, week or month. That's not to say that there's no place for 'one and done' actions (as we saw from Chapter 4, the power of getting things done is testament to how we move through life), but they help us get a feeling of accomplishment or control, first and foremost, rather than nurturing.

Assuming you have some kind of list of activities, ask yourself why you want to do each of them. Actually, I want you to ask yourself why *at least three times*. Stay with me on this one.

I used to work in media relations, which meant I spent a lot of time working with heads of organizations to help them pitch their stories to journalists. One of the most common challenges they faced was that they couldn't explain what the point of their organization was. They'd tell me *what* they did and *how* they did it, but they really struggled to explain *why* they did it. So, I'd get them to tell me what they did, and then I'd ask them: 'Why?' They'd get a bit flustered and give me an answer. So, then I'd ask them 'Why?' again. They'd usually look at me with pained exasperation, and give me a slightly deeper answer. And then I'd ask them 'Why?' one more time. By this point they were ready to throttle me, but it had the effect of getting beneath the surface – to the part where purpose resides.

Let's take an example from my own list to show how this works:

What: Reading in bed with a cup of tea.
Why: Because I get to zone out.
But why: Because taking time for reading fills my energy reserves back up.
But really, why: Because being fully charged makes me a more loving partner and parent.

Knowing that I want to show up for my family with love establishes the purpose of something I will instinctively reach for, given the time and opportunity, but otherwise struggle to protect or explain within the daily grind. When you look at it this way, the choice is no longer between bleaching your toilet or reading a book, but between bleaching your toilet or showing up for your family. I know what I'd rather be doing.

There are no hard and fast requirements for what you do to nurture yourself, but there must always be a purpose. When we develop a narrative for why we do things, we give them meaning; and when we give them meaning, we turbocharge their effectiveness. This is because our narratives help personalize our actions, which makes them even more relevant to our identity, and when we do something that is focused on us, not someone else, we're more likely to believe it will be effective. A long-term study by Louisiana Tech University in 2014 showed that people who demonstrated greater authenticity during the first research period were more satisfied with their lives when they were recontacted months later. It just goes to show that each opportunity we get to express and take care of ourselves creates impact far beyond that single moment in time.

For your pleasure

After I'd dated myself for an entire weekend, I started to notice the difference between satisfaction and pleasure in the kinds of activities I did at home and beyond. My routines were about getting things done successfully, like working out or cooking a meal, so the output was important to me (calories burned, food on a plate). What I observed in things that started to look more like rituals was that there wasn't strictly a defined output. The doing was, in and of itself, the thing that became the pleasure. We saw from the *Life at Home* research in 2021 that one in four people felt that doing hobbies or personal projects was important to their overall mental well-being, reflecting the sense that the experience they got from 'doing' was the important part.

When it comes to what kinds of activities you might choose to do as you reflect on the purpose of your nurturing rituals, there are two simple approaches – and you can start with either or combine them both:

- Do the things which give you the most pleasure whilst you are doing them
- Do the things you've always done as routine but reframe them as rituals

There's an easy 'sniff test' for pleasure. If you find yourself mildly dreading the thing you've said you'll do every Wednesday evening, it's not a ritual – it's an obligation. I never talk about 'guilty pleasures' because I don't think we should ever feel guilty about doing something which makes us feel good. When we experience pleasure, we're tapping into a deep part of ourselves, and we're soothing and holding space for our needs. When we experience pleasure, we cannot be anything but utterly authentic. If the ritual feels perfunctory or tedious or burdensome, then you've lost sight of pleasure and you're moving away from your authentic self.

Another great way into this is to reflect on whether you have any hobbies. Remember that feeling of uninterrupted joy when you were immersed in something you loved to do as a kid? As adults, we all too often leave hobbies behind, as life is filled with responsibilities and work. I used to act and dance and sing in choirs, all of which gave me enormous pleasure and nurtured me deeply, but I struggle to reconcile doing these things as a fully grown adult because I fear they might appear childish or amateur. Learning about people's hobbies through the *Life at Home* research has given me a new vantage point into leisure activities, with a welcome reminder that the whole point of a hobby is that it's not about excellence or professionalism. I get tired hearing that we should all be turning our 'side hustles' into paid opportunities, like we have to squeeze out compensation for the time we spend doing anything at all or we're devaluing ourselves. Leave the side hustles be. Hobbies are about the pleasure of doing, taking time for yourself, learning and having fun. Your hobbies might involve going to a class or participating in a formal group activity, but almost anything you give yourself over to in the moment could be classed as a hobby: reading, gardening, writing, drawing, listening to podcasts, baking and so on. And yes, watching TV with a glass of wine definitely counts as a hobby.

The second way into rituals is to reframe the routines you currently perform for yourself in the running of your domestic life. Consider routines where you already have opportunities to work with the senses which can tap into your pleasure receptors, like smell, taste and touch. Again, this is not about the routines which are in service to other people or cracking through your life admin. You want to work with the moments in the day when you're taking the time, no matter how constrained, to attend to yourself. Overall, there's a curious gender split here, given that women are far more likely to prioritize self-care than men are – 24 per cent compared to just 9 per cent. This speaks to the differences in how we assign value to self-care, which is why it's so important to establish the 'why' of our nurturing actions. It's also helpful to look at things we all do, regardless of gender and perceptions of self-care, as the basis of our rituals. Examples include getting ready for the day, eating meals, winding down from the day and getting ready for bed.

Let's examine that last one, given we've already established that sleep is more effective when we consider it a ritual. If we layer in my example of purpose from the previous solution, when I asked 'why', then we can start to flesh out a story that establishes that getting a good night's sleep will make me a more loving partner and parent.

If we had some kind of a heat map for the typical bedtime routines encountered through the *Life at Home* research, I reckon we'd see the following hot spots of concern:

- Too much screen time in the hours before bed
- Going to bed too late to ensure a full night's sleep
- Brains on overdrive churning through mental 'to-do' lists and worries
- Patchy and inconsistent ways to prepare for bed
- Disturbances through the night

Do you recognize some of those hot spots in your own bedtime routine? You might feel like they are mostly unavoidable, but I want to assure you that the process of going to bed each night can be something that deeply nurtures you, rather than a last-minute bookend to an exhausting day. To help, I'd like to share some bedtime rituals I use when I need to attend to myself.

If I have to wake up at 6 a.m. and I want eight hours' sleep, I need to be asleep by 10 p.m. Working backwards, this might include:

- Putting my screens away by 9 p.m. at the latest and dimming the lights around the home
- Writing in my journal to process the day and noting any actions for the following one
- Leaving my mobile phone charging outside of the bedroom overnight
- Taking the day off with calming, scented products and taking some extra time to massage my face and scalp
- Putting on clean pyjamas
- Dropping a few drops of lavender oil on to my pillow and taking three deep breaths in and out
- Giving myself half an hour of reading time in bed before lights-out
- Making time for a cuddle with my husband (for the PG rating of this solution)

Life gets in the way, of course. For all the will in the world, I cannot stop my children from needing me in the middle of the night or alleviate the pressures placed on working families that eat into every available minute. All too often, bedtime is a scramble for the finish line and I'll make a weary calculation of what's left for me in those twenty-four hours as the clock ticks closer to midnight. But when I hold space for bedtime rituals on any given night, I know I'm choosing to show up for myself and my family the following day.

A time and a place for everything

There's a time and a place for everything, and that includes your rituals. By this, I mean that identifying where in your home you do your ritual, when it takes place and for how long will help you honour your need for it. Broadly speaking, rituals need two contextual things:

- A supportive environment
- The safety of a boundary

For all the reasons that routines are easy to establish in the home, so too are rituals. They benefit enormously from dedicated spaces and places where we can store and access equipment easily, making the decision to step into a ritual as frictionless as possible. The kinds of zoning solutions we explored in Chapter 4 as a way to dial up the feeling of accomplishment come into play here. If your ritual is meditation before bedtime, for example, then make a pact with yourself that you'll use a certain part of your home to do this every time. It's one less thing to think about, and you can make sure everything you need for your ritual is readily to hand. I also use this approach to remind myself of the purpose, by walking into the space where I intend to practise a ritual and saying my intention out loud (or under my breath, so my family don't think I've finally lost the plot). Fake it till you make it, they say – this applies to rituals too, where we state our intention into being.

As I touched on earlier, some people struggle to get into the right mindset for rituals, or any kind of relaxation, if there's too much clutter in the space around them or chores to be done. I can be quite particular about relaxing in my living room when my kids have gone to bed, which can only happen if all their toys have been cleared away. Tidying them up helps me shift gears from Mum Mode to Me Mode. If you find it difficult to accommodate self-care when you have a finite amount of time and a stack of domestic chores to do first, then I'd like to suggest a small hack which works well for me:

> → **Rather than view the chores as a barrier, treat them as a runway**
> Set a timer for anywhere between ten minutes and an hour, and crack through your chores as quickly as possible. As soon as the buzzer goes, you accept that you have done enough and move into your ritual.

I find that twenty minutes is my sweet spot – you can get a hell of a lot done in that time, especially if you focus on the space where you want to spend your hard-won me-time. The whole exercise also gives you a little dopamine boost from accomplishing something specific within a deadline, which is a gratifying way to step into self-care.

Boundaries are a more slippery thing. We resonate with the intention of a ritual when we're in the right headspace, which means – as we discussed in Chapter 2, in relation to privacy – that the boundary we place around our ritual is only there if we feel it is. Clutter and chores are one thing, but interruptions, disturbances or – far, far worse – someone dismissing your nurturing ritual as something trivial, are something else. Scheduling your ritual and giving yourself a timeframe for it will help you establish clear boundaries, and it will also help give you the fortitude to prioritize the ritual over other demands on your time. Telling people what you are doing can also set some helpful expectations about what you need (silence; no interruptions) and even turn it into more of an event.

Why not go a step further and give your ritual a name? There are many traditional rituals around the world that people enjoy, such as the Tea Ceremony in Japan, where simply saying the name of the ritual conjures up a sense that these actions hold power. I have a list of tried-and-tested stand-alone rituals I turn to when life feels a bit too overwhelming, which my friends and family laughingly refer to as 'aggressive self-care'. One of these rituals is eating a really fancy cake in bed whilst I stream a show I've watched a hundred times already. It's just pure pleasure. All I need to say is 'It's time for Cake in Bed' and everyone knows what's at stake. Talking about your Morning Ritual or your Evening Ritual (or your Cake in Bed Ritual) will lend an air of time-honoured tradition to your actions, making it much easier to reach out when you need them.

Isabella and I ended up living together for well over a year, and I'd say that we obtained something resembling domestic harmony in the end. One of the ways we found each other was by doing something outside the apartment together: running. When I was at a loss as to how to spend my spare time in the wake of the break-up, I signed up for a women's 5k around Hyde Park simply so I would have something to do in the evenings that wasn't frantically stalking my ex-boyfriend on social media. I got the bug, and before long Isabella and I had signed up for a 10k – and then I was off to the races, literally, with a half-marathon and then, against all the odds, a full one. Running around our neighbourhood in all kinds of weather came to be another significant ritual for me – one that reached out into the extended home and brought me back again with renewed energy, patience and contentment. It's one I readily returned to years later when I had the opportunity, as I mentioned when elaborating on accomplishment and the power of accountability. When I met James, the man who would become my husband, I told him I liked to run around the park a few times a week. He started joining me, too, and said it helped him get to know me better in the early days of our relationship. By sharing my ritual, I was sharing who I was.

Much of what I have covered in this chapter is focused on you, the individual, and your need for nurturing yourself at home. Of course, many rituals in our daily lives include other people, and these are also excellent examples of how we can attend to ourselves in the context of the people around us. When rituals bring their arms around a group of people, they foster belonging – by honouring a ritual together, we are telling someone that we care about them and want to connect with them. I was struck by a piece of research that Bruce Feiler referenced in his book *The Secrets of Happy Families*, which was a wide-ranging survey conducted by the University of Michigan over sixteen years. It showed that the amount of time that children spent eating meals at home was the single biggest predictor of academic achievement and behavioural problems. As he wrote, 'Mealtime was more influential than time spent in school, studying, attending religious services, or playing sports.' We must not underestimate the power of rituals, let alone the power of rituals at home.

I want to go back to Katherine May's excellent point about how unfashionable it appears to administer self-care, because there will always be people around you who will buck against your actions. There will be moments when a friend pulls a funny face when they hear of your nightly rituals, no matter if it's using a sheet mask or practising transcendental meditation with a side of gong therapy. Parents might pass judgement about what is a 'valuable use of your time', and partners may – with good reason – call you back when you slouch off to bed with a book, leaving a stack of dishes and two mewling children behind. Stay firm on what you need. They'll all see the light eventually.

Yes, it's hard to stand up for yourself. But it's harder still to live a life without nurturing.

7

Joy

'Joy is not made to be a crumb.'

Mary Oliver, 'Don't Hesitate'

ONE OF MY MOST JOYFUL memories is the day I moved into a small flat within spitting distance of the bucolic Hampstead Heath in London with James, a little over a year into our relationship. Lugging furniture and boxes up several flights of dilapidated stairs doesn't typically fire off a load of endorphins, especially when we realized what a state the place was in once we'd crossed the threshold. But the pleasure was in what we were creating together, from that first moving day onwards.

A cursory look around revealed that the apartment was, quite literally, falling apart. The wooden stairs from the street to the front door were rotten from the ground up and swayed underfoot. The glass in the bedroom window was cracked and the frame so water-damaged that the curtains constantly moved in the breeze. There was black mould in the bathroom and moths in the carpet. Once we were living there, we had to make an almost weekly call-out to the plumbers to remove the gunk that gathered in the long outflow pipe beneath the kitchen, their high-pressure work leaving a ghostly imprint of fat cascading down from the gutter outside. That home was a crumbling black hole into which we poured obscene amounts of money on rent, but my overwhelming sensation when I think back to those years is that it gave me endless joy.

Experiencing joy is no more complicated than the simple act of taking great pleasure in things. It's a state of mind triggered by events or situations which are fun or pleasurable or rewarding. The feeling that we get is actually a series of chemical messages your brain sends around your body, including serotonin and dopamine, which can do things like raise a particular kind of smile out of you that no other feeling can create. It's really good for you, this thing that elicits your inner Cheshire Cat, given that the feeling of joy is linked to major physiological and psychological changes which benefit our overall health. And it's no small fry, either, given that a range of different studies have demonstrated that experiencing joy can boost our immune system, help pain management and even increase our lifespan.

Just like the feeling of accomplishment, which we explored in Chapter 4, the need for joy at home wasn't something people talked about until we started hearing about it in the 2021 IKEA research home visits, after the Covid-19 pandemic. Until there was a deadly airborne virus to contend with, I suppose a lot of us went out to have a good time and home was just where we slept off the hangover. But needs change, and a reckoning was due. Ever since we started tracking it, in 2022, nine in ten people have said finding enjoyment at home is important – but as with the other emotional needs, far fewer regularly feel it where they live. This deficit of domestic joy, at 36 per cent overall, is one of the largest emotional gaps. Which begs the question: Who wants to live in a home that can't even raise a smile out of them?

Writing about joy is hard to do without also writing about happiness and pleasure. In my mind, they are part and parcel of how we live and look back on A Good Life. Far deeper thinkers and writers than I have tussled with these very topics, coaxing out the different ways they show up in the world. I quite like the way J. D. Salinger captured it in one of his short stories: 'The fact is always obvious much too late, but the most singular difference between happiness and joy is that happiness is a solid and joy a liquid.' It gets to something of the impossibility of nailing joy to the ground.

Someone who knows a lot about joy and her states is Meik Wiking, CEO and founder of the Happiness Research Institute in Copenhagen. He burst into our lives with his bestselling call to arms, *The Little Book of Hygge*, which helped popularize that Danish notion of 'cosiness' I discussed in Chapter 5. Wiking is steeped in the research of happiness, and has written extensively about how to create more joy in your everyday life. I am particularly taken by his exploration of what he calls 'memory triggers', in his more recent book, *The Art of Making Memories*, as simple devices to help create and capture happy, joyful moments. Wiking believes that perfectly ordinary experiences have the potential to feel joyful, and many of them take place at home, like eating meals, watching films, playing board games, celebrating the small wins of everyday life, and so on. His point is that by being more deliberate in our actions, we can experience enjoyment in the moment and establish a lifetime of joyful memories.

Reflecting on this whilst looking back at the kind of actions and experiences that people have tagged with 'joy' through the IKEA *Life at Home* research home visits, it's clear that the potential for more enjoyment sits with three distinct drivers:

1. How we learn to **anticipate** joy.
2. How we set **intentions** for joyful experiences.
3. How we pay **attention** to joyful experiences, both in the moment and afterwards.

Responding to these aspects, I have devised some 'hands and heart' solutions which address the way we can enable more joy at home and how to honour it afterwards. This is meaningful work and more timely than ever in this volatile world. Even if we're not facing stay-at-home measures, the *Life at Home* research tells us people are cutting back on the expense of hobbies and activities outside the home due to the rising cost of living. All told, we're turning to our home for happiness more than ever. Equipped with these small but powerful solutions for all kinds of living situations, I believe that each and every one of us has the opportunity to unlock so much joy in our life at home – even during the times when things feel hard.

Before I lived with James, I'd not typically seen where I lived as a canvas for joy. It's not that I was unhappy in all those other homes – far from it – it's just that I was more preoccupied with the joy that bubbled up beyond the front door. But with my life firmly nested in this flat with James, I'd turn the corner on to our road after a particularly gruelling commute back from work and my heart would flutter with expectant delight at the sight of our flat, with its rotten windowsills and crumbling plasterwork.

This place was home to big joyful moments – birthdays, Halloween, Christmas and 'just because . . .' parties. It was home to my wedding day preparations, with my hair in curlers at the kitchen table whilst one of my heavily pregnant bridesmaids soaked in the bath and we all sang Dolly Parton songs. But, more importantly, this place was home to small joyful moments too. Those countless dinners with friends, the visits from loved ones, the afternoons spent doing the crossword with a foot rub, and watching films with wine and popcorn. Looking back, I can see that there was an intentionality to these smaller acts. There was a desire to make the everyday thrum with happiness – to turn a meal into a moment, or a task into an event.

I wanted to go beyond the pleasure of a ritual and into that vital feeling that rises up from your heart and on to your face.

The IKEA *Life at Home* Report from 2023 confirms that it's typically these much smaller moments that bring people the biggest feeling of joy, with 35 per cent globally saying that hugs with a loved one brings them the most joy at home. For people with pets, just watching them sleep ranks in the top most joyful moments at home across many countries – something I can firmly attest to as I lovingly gaze upon my incredibly large and entitled housecat, who naps for more than eighteen hours a day. And yet, for all the ways in which people point to accessible acts of joy, like snoring dogs, we just cannot shake this persistent emotional gap. What gives? I believe the problem starts with whether or not we anticipate joy in our daily lives.

Anticipating joy

Looking back at all the emotional needs we've covered so far, I can't help but think that joy is all too often the one for which we give up personal responsibility. Perhaps we think that the cosmos decides when joy comes to us, and we have no say over when or how it might arise. Or perhaps, much like some of the challenges around nurturing, we do not think we are worthy enough for it.

The first thing I want to say is that everyone is deserving of joy. The second thing is that getting to joy shouldn't feel like another chore on our to-do list, when we already have so much to do just to keep the lights on. For parents in particular, there's a kind of anxiety that we need to make home as joyful as possible for our kids, and that we should be committed to creating core memories they'll draw on in years to come. I lump it together with the impossible comparisons we continually make, between ourselves and other people living in vastly different places, which I raised in Chapter 1.

During the Covid-19 pandemic – truly, the litmus test for all of our emotional needs – many people felt that their home had to do so much that there was simply no time or space for joy once the essentials had been accounted for. And yet, many of the kinds of lockdown activities people got on with – like the ones I talked about when we explored accomplishment in Chapter 4 – were also testament to the smaller kind of joy. Without any elaborate expenditure or event management, people were bringing little acts of happiness into their domestic lives. Baking with their kids, chatting to friends online, playing the guitar with their flatmate, restaging masterpiece paintings using random objects around the home . . . It says a lot about the human need for pleasure that during this dark time, when we were separated from our loved ones and crippled with grief and anxiety, there were so many people who dug deep and found huge reserves of domestic joy in the everyday.

Cultivating joy appears to be easier for some people than for others, but the good news is that everyone can learn how to create physical and mental space for it. When we are proactive in our approach to joy, we learn how to anticipate something enjoyable happening, and when we anticipate that enjoyable thing in the future, we also feel joy in the present. If you think about it, anticipatory joy is a real win-win because you get to feel joy twice. The Germans have a word for it (of course they do), *Vorfreude*, which translates literally as 'before joy', along with the snappy aphorism that '*Vorfreude ist die beste Freude*' (anticipation is the best joy).

When I tuck my daughter up at night, once her baby brother has drifted off, she usually has a litany of wild questions ranging from 'Why is the moon in the sky?' to 'Where is all the blood in my body?', which I often assume is stealth prevarication from having to go to sleep. But there's one question she always asks: 'What will we do in the morning?' By this point, I am on my knees with exhaustion and desperate for the questions to end so I can slope out of her room and get horizontal on the sofa. My daughter will not accept glib answers, like 'Get dressed' or 'Go to kindergarten', so she'll push for more details until she is satisfied that she's got plenty to look forward to the next day. Lately, I've started thinking that this particular question is less about delaying sleep and more about anticipatory joy. And it's forced me to rethink how I take a run-up to the next day myself. So, my first solution is an easy one, inspired by my daughter:

> → **Before you go to bed at night, think about one thing you're looking forward to at home the following day**
> It could be something very simple, like your first coffee of the day, or something that feels more of a moment, like a friend coming over for lunch. Give yourself a minute to visualize it in your mind, then let the *Vorfreude* work its magic.

I've noticed that if I tell my daughter we'll make something special for breakfast, like pancakes (her favourite meal), she'll literally squeal with glee into her pillow. It's such a great thing to anticipate because it's in the very near future, so there's all the more reason to go to sleep. Seeing her anticipatory joy never fails to raise a smile in me when I think about how much she'll enjoy those pancakes – and how much I'll get to enjoy them too.

Making pancakes is usually something I have to plan for, however, because it requires certain ingredients and enough time. I can speak from experience when I say that there's nothing worse than promising pancakes and then having to make a grumpy shuffle to the supermarket because you don't have enough milk. Organized fun might sound like the death knell for joy, and the kind of thing an extremely chill Type-A person like me might recommend, but bear with me when I say that there is joy to be found in planning. Here's an exercise to help you out:

→ **Make a plan for three fun things you can do at home in the coming month**
You don't need any project management tools for this – just a pen and paper, or a few notes on your phone. Maybe you can plan a romantic dinner for your partner, a games afternoon with your kids, or a movie marathon with friends. Use the planning as an opportunity to get into the flow of anticipation – what will you eat, play or watch? Who will you invite over? Is there something fun you want to try for the first time? Even a few minutes in a time-strapped day thinking about plans for something fun in the future can give you a little boost of anticipatory joy.

By getting ready for happy experiences in our everyday lives, we start to create a mindset which is primed to establish joyful experiences in our lives at home. This is a fantastic baseline for the next two drivers of joy.

Setting our intentions

I can plan and prepare all manner of elaborate activities for my four-year-old daughter, whilst her little brother happily gnaws away on a teething ring, but left to her own devices at home, she is hardwired to play – tea parties for teddies, selling ice creams from her kitchen, making a Lego castle, dressing up as Elton John (we have a lot of elaborate toy sunglasses), and so on. The thing I love most about watching my daughter play is how joyful she appears. She's simply not thinking about anything or anyone else. She's not preoccupied with that terse email she got from a colleague whilst she sets up the cups and saucers, or running through a shopping list whilst she pours her Lego bricks on to the floor. She doesn't worry about anyone judging her whilst she babbles along to showtunes. She's in the zone. I think we can all learn something from this.

In addition to the *Life at Home* Report, IKEA has also undertaken extensive research into the importance of play. Over the years, the research has repeatedly shown that play is critical for a better life at home. When we think about people playing, it's usually accompanied by a mental image of a child surrounded by toys, like my daughter. But the research shows that play is actually a mindset rather than a specific set of activities. Play is a way of finding fun and joy in everything we do, which means it's not just for kids – it's for adults, too. This means that if you want to find more joy at home, a great place to start is by getting playful.

There are certain characteristics to play which mark it out from other activities. The problem is that as soon as you try to put your hands around it, play just slips away. It's why I'm not a fan of using play as a proxy to do other things, like learning your times tables or tidying up. The minute a playful activity strays into goal-setting and anything remotely serious, it might knock on the door of some other needs – like accomplishment or control – but it's not going to give us unfettered enjoyment. For play to walk and talk and dance with joy, it needs to stay lighthearted, satisfying, active, and – here's the nut to crack – spontaneous. Contrary to what I've said about organized fun, that last quality feels all but impossible if we're all busy planning joy so we can anticipate it ... So, let's zoom back out to the bigger picture.

The conditions for joy to take root typically have to overcome two recurring barriers:

* **Our physical environment**
  When our home is not optimized to *experience* joy.

* **Our headspace**
  When we are not in the right frame of mind to *receive* joy.

How can we maximize these qualities of play to help us leapfrog our barriers to joy and become more intentional about something that's supposed to just magically happen on its own? The answer lies in how we ready our homes and ourselves.

We'll start with our physical environment.

A lot of us seem to hold back from fully releasing into joyful experiences at home because we've told ourselves it's too hard / messy / time-consuming / burdensome / expensive ... You name it, I've thought it. The good news is I've also seen how small changes and additions to the home can better accommodate joyful activities. Let's go back to those pancakes I promised my daughter we'd make in the morning.

I didn't always enjoy making pancakes. For quite a while, I resented the fact I would have to crawl out of bed whilst everyone else cosied up under the duvet – until I realized my daughter also really wanted to help make the pancakes. Initially, it was too much to contemplate. I wasn't sure how much of the batter would end up in the pan, and I knew I'd be wiping it from every kitchen surface for the rest of the morning. Solo, I could get those American-style pancake stacks out in twenty minutes – but with an erratic sous-chef, I was looking at a solid forty-five. And I was already projecting to the almighty clean-up which loomed ahead of me, skipping right past the part where my daughter delighted in breaking eggs and using the whisk. The tally against joy was high: messy, time-consuming, burdensome ... check, check, check. I had it all the wrong way round.

So, I made a few minor adjustments to reliably prime the task for joy. Specifically, I put in place a few simple actions which make things run a bit smoother:

> **Get the right tools**
> Along with having already stocked up on all the right ingredients to make the pancakes, I let my daughter get to work using unsmashable implements that don't leave me lurking next to her like a wet sack of anxiety. I specifically bought her a small pink spatula for baking, so she has her own tool to work with that keeps her happily entertained.

> → **Specify roles and responsibilities**
> I gratefully delegate the breakfast clean-up to my husband. If there's batter on the floor, the wall or the ceiling, he's the pro at dealing with it.

Do you recognize a few joy-killers in your own experiences? If so, I want you to think about **three things that stop you from doing something fun at home**. And then I want you to take **one action that would make it easier to do**. To help you, here are some of the most common causes of frustration at home which we have repeatedly seen through the *Life at Home* research, along with my suggestions:

> → **Clearing and cleaning:** This is a *big* one, topping the list of regular frustrations at home. This is especially challenging if an activity is messy or chaotic, which cooking or any kind of craft invariably is. I suggest delegating cleaning responsibilities to everyone involved and making clearing up part of the activity. Designating parts of the home where certain messy activities take place is also helpful, along with having a dedicated box or cupboard stashed with wipe-down covers for tables and floors and all the appropriate cleaning materials.
>
> → **Organizing our stuff:** Not knowing where things live around the home, so they're easy

to access, is also in the top three global frustrations points. In high-volume areas, like the kitchen, which has food, gadgets and implements, this can be acutely aggravating. If you regularly need the same set of tools, ingredients or implements for a certain activity, try storing them in the same place, so you can access them in one go when you want them.

→ **Time:** We have so little of it with tight schedules to stick to, and people and responsibilities to take care of. It's hard to slice up even more for the fun stuff. I've talked about zoning activities to a certain part of the house, but you can also zone them to a certain time of day or week to make planning easier. What you might lose in spontaneity you gain in anticipation. When time is crunched but you don't want to be the person that's clock-watching, setting a timer (even if it's just for two minutes) helps everyone know when to shift focus without someone feeling like the Fun Police.

Being intentional about joy doesn't mean an activity needs to be elaborate. In fact, it's frequently the opposite. Most often the smallest of intentions can unlock unexpectedly joyful moments. Eliminating points of friction helps us execute our planned fun, but it's also possible to cultivate our environments for spontaneous fun. I have a basket of blankets and throws in the living room, which makes it easier to snuggle up on the sofa or build a 'fort'. We've got linen napkins and candles near the dining table so my husband and I can turn any meal, whether it's pancakes or poussin, into something instantly more *hygge*. I have friends who keep frozen cookie dough on hand to enjoy a fresh batch in under ten minutes. And a colleague once told me she always has a bottle of champagne in the fridge, so there's no excuse not to celebrate when the occasion demands it.

Maybe your spontaneity hack is a well-positioned lamp with a warm light for reading together, or a smooth-flowing pen that sits snugly in your hand for some alone-time with the crossword. Maybe it's something as simple as a fully charged laptop for streaming a classic romcom, or a magazine rack by the sofa for digging into back copies of the *New Yorker* when the moment allows. You know the things that get a smile out of you, so prime your way to access them as intentionally – and playfully – as possible.

With our home environment primed, we need to turn our attention to our **mental state**. Most of my mental distractions pile up towards the end of the day, after hours of shoving things in my brain and energy leaking out of my body. I'd wager that most of us find it easier to feel joyful on a Saturday morning after eight hours of sleep than on a Wednesday evening after eight hours of meetings.

So how can we get our heads in the game when we want to be open to more joyful experiences at home, at any time of the day? Here are a few tried-and-tested ways to help manage your mental energy:

> → **Put your phone away**
> Establish a timeframe for when you are offline (between 7 p.m. and 7 a.m., say), and stick to it. Being unavailable remotely brings you into the real world. One of my research colleagues once told me he puts his mobile phone in an old biscuit tin as soon as he stops work, which is a signal to him – and his loved ones – that he's mentally present at precisely the time his family wants his attention the most.
>
> → **Schedule things which are draining**
> Two great examples of this are drawing up meal plans and cleaning rotas. Knowing what you're putting on the table and who's responsible for cleaning up every day, without having to freestyle the answers, is *liberating*. It's also an area where research shows a clear gender split, with women typically three times as likely as men to say they are frustrated by doing domestic chores. Without the burden of domestic life nibbling at your availability, you free yourself up for a lot more spontaneous joy.

> **→ Get rid of the garbage**
> Sometimes you need to take out the trash – mentally speaking. Taking a walk around the block, lying down for ten minutes in a dark room, running a hot shower ... There's no right or wrong way, just your way. You can't get to the goods until you've got rid of the garbage, so take a beat to clear your head to let you open up to joy.

These hacks are great ways to be mentally present for joy in daily and domestic ways, but I also want to touch on a bigger mental challenge to enjoyment that many of us sit with but struggle to explain: foreboding joy. As the name suggests, it's all the way at the other end of the spectrum to the much more delightful *Vorfreude*. I first came across foreboding joy in the work of Brené Brown, specifically in her books *The Gifts of Imperfection* and *Daring Greatly*. She describes foreboding joy as being afraid to lean into joy because you 'find yourself waiting for the other shoe to drop'. Meaning, we're all waiting for a seemingly inevitable event to take place which will take our joy away from us.

I think a lot of us are worried that bringing joy into our lives will also usher in disaster, like some kind of cosmic redistribution. According to Brown, 95 per cent of parents involved in her research experience foreboding joy with their children. *Oh boy.* I know what it's like to watch my children in full, joyful flow with their toys and teddies, before my mind suddenly lurches towards unmitigated tragedy and the thought of losing them. It's one hell of a way to poison the well.

The answer, says Brown, is gratitude. The one consistent trait amongst people who are better equipped at stopping foreboding joy in its tracks is regular appreciation for what they have, not what they fear they might lose. In Chapter 1, I provided an exercise that can help you establish your own gratitude anchors. If you suffer from foreboding joy, reach for your anchors to bring you back home. This brings us full circle to the data we have on what gives people the most joy: hugs and snoring dogs. Perhaps the easiest way to get back to joy in these kinds of moments is simply to take an extra beat and give a small nod of thanks that we have people, pets and other particulars in our home with which to build a joyful life.

Paying attention

With our intentions set, we can turn our minds to attention. Did you really experience joy if you can't remember it? Being able to recall a moment of joy in your life is the definition of a happy memory, and happy memories make for a joyful life.

Casting back further to the root of so much of my own joy today, I can see that many of my abiding memories involve eating together with my family – both during my childhood and more recently with my own brood. My father is no happier than when he's standing in a kitchen, listening to music whilst he dredges things in flour and egg and roughs up potatoes on a baking sheet. Food is my father's love language. There is no event too small to merit a joyful browse round the fishmonger and market stalls, where he will literally rub his hands with glee at the prospect of scallops for a starter or ripe tomatoes for his side salad.

I can recall any number of family meals, not because of anything extraordinary that happened at the time but because we revisit them so often when we are all together. These happy recollections are oral histories, recalled and retold, which is what renders, colours and cements the memory for each of us. I can regularly time-travel back to these moments because we all paid them attention in the days, months and then years that came after. This is why my joyful memories from the crumbling flat down the road from Hampstead Heath are so clear, despite having very few photographs from that time. To this day, my husband and I regale one another with stories stretching back fifteen years and counting.

Preparing and sharing food is one of the easiest ways to increase the feeling of joy at home. It's a simple backdrop to the thing that as many as one in three of us say is the best thing about getting together: laughing with friends. Research shows that eating food together creates more pleasure than eating food alone, and sharing food is even more effective. When we eat family-style, passing dishes and condiments around the table, we attend to the people around us and the food itself. This simple action helps us reach the third driver for joy – paying attention to joyful experiences – and it's something you can practise in the moment as well as after an event.

Going back to the 'memory triggers' that Meik Wiking recommends, we can consciously curate experiences or activities with these triggers factored in so they're easier to remember later. This technique is a great way to create joyful memories in your home, because you're in daily reach of various ephemera that will trigger the nostalgia.

> → **When you're next planning something you're looking forward to at home, think about including a unique memory trigger as part of the activity**
>
> It could be a chipped and time-worn serving dish for a Sunday lunch with family, or a specific mug for hot chocolate when you set up a cosy movie marathon with the kids. Using the senses, why not designate a specific song when you're packing for a holiday or a certain scented candle when you invite friends over for drinks? Whatever you include, it'll have the effect of reminding you about the fun things you did whenever you see, hear or smell the relevant memory trigger – and prompt you to do those fun things again.

Another way of using objects to trigger memories is to keep something from a particular moment in time and bring it into your home. As I've mentioned before from the *Life at Home* research, people who see themselves reflected back in their home are more likely to feel positive about where they live and view home as a source of well-being. And we're better able to see ourselves represented where we live if we're surrounded by identity markers, especially objects that are visual stand-ins for various stories from our lives.

> → **When you experience something that brings you joy, think about an object that can represent that memory, then showcase it in your home**
>
> It's tempting to assume a photograph can do that for us, but the beauty of a more abstract object is that it acts as a prompt rather than an official record. Consider taking a stone from the beach where you had a lovely picnic before your kids buried you up to your neck in the sand. Or maybe dry some flowers from the day you spent in the park with friends when you lost track of time and got locked in. Maybe it's the setlist your favourite band gave you when you heard them live at a bar, or a funny little painting you picked up from a flea market when a morning coffee turned into a walk across the length of the city and sundown cocktails. These are souvenirs from places where there isn't a tourist shop.

In addition to prompts we can curate and cultivate at home, another research-backed way to enhance the feeling of joy is to write about it. I do this as much as I can by writing in my journal most evenings, no matter the substance or feeling of the day. I find that poring back through the pages every now and then is a gorgeous exercise for revisiting the joy I've frequently felt, acknowledging that these moments coexist with sad or hard times too. This gives me a small hit of the good stuff all over again just thinking about it, and a welcome reminder that joy is always possible to find even when things feel tough. For all that I might be tussling with on any given day, there are golden nuggets of joy in every week to remember.

I know that journaling or keeping a diary isn't for everyone, and it can often feel like another chore at the end of the day. For those tendencies, I have two other suggestions:

> → **Tell someone about something fun you did**
> Asking everyone in your household over dinner to share something fun they did that day is an easy way of opening up the discussion. You can also talk about the fun you had last time you did something as you make plans for when to do it again, like dressing up for a seasonal activity (I like to think about Halloween a good six months in advance) or what you'd like to do during an upcoming holiday.

> → **Put the photos where you can find them**
> I don't know about you, but I have so many photos on my phone that I am paralyzed with exhaustion just thinking about what to do with them all. To make some inroads, I've started choosing ten snaps from every month, printing them out and popping them in a nice book at the end of the year. When I'm in need of a joy boost, I pluck one of the books at random and look through it, and I always feel that Cheshire Cat grin spreading from cheek to cheek. The point is that physical photo albums don't have to be reserved for special occasions, like weddings or expensive holidays. The daily joy in your life at home could fill an album every year for the rest of your life.

Paying attention to moments of joy is how we bank them for life. When we're faced with so many distractions, from managers pinging us emails at all hours, to toddlers making constant demands for snacks, we would do well to remember something Meik Wiking wrote that hit me in the gut: 'Our lives are not the days that have passed, but the days we will remember forever.'

Anticipation, intention and attention are how we bring joy into our lives in the long term. It's also how we pass it between generations. This is the most powerful legacy of joy at home.

Watching my father in the kitchen is how I learned to cook, though he never explicitly taught me. Standing beside him at the stove is how I decompressed from school. I'd chatter about my day, and my father would pull the beards off mussels or salt some pork whilst I looked on. The sense-memories of handling various ingredients would come to me many years later, when I'd find myself stepping up to the literal plate to take on the task of preparing *moules marinières* or spatchcocking a chicken whilst my flatmates blanched in panic, thumbing through some TV chef's latest cookery book filled with recipes they'd never dare try.

Recently I found myself fretting about the random contents of my fridge once again, as I contemplated making a family-friendly dinner on a drizzly Tuesday evening. The threads of routine had loosened and we hadn't meal-planned that week, but I knew I had half a chicken left over from Sunday lunch, which could be the foundation for any number of great meals, just as I'd observed and learned. As I started to pull the meat off the bones, my fingers slick with grease, I thought of my father. He'd be triumphantly gnawing on the gristle by now, thrilled at finding a whole new meal in the aftermath of the one before. 'Dinner is going to be a bit hodgepodge,' I warned my husband as he ventured over. 'Oh, come on – you love it,' he replied. 'You're just like your dad, foraging through the leftovers.' I couldn't help but smile – he was right, of course, despite my grumbling.

I threw the meat together with the remains of a

jar of pesto and the last dregs of a tub of cream, and boiled up half a packet of pasta. When everything came together in my favourite serving dish, I grated an old heel of parmesan over the lot to finish. Hardly fine dining, but that was never the intention. After serving up, with linen napkins and a few candles, we chatted about our day and what we wanted to do at the weekend. I watched my children laughingly drop pasta on the floor, knowing one of us would have to get down on our hands and knees to pick it up at some point, but it didn't matter. At that moment, I was with the people I love the most, sharing dinner and stories around our time-worn dining table, in our own home. Just like when I was a kid.

When you consider the ways that joy finds a home in your home, I'd like you to think about how you hand that joy over to others too. We might be able to tweak our own methods for memories, but it's nearly impossible to ensure the people we love and care for will always remember the same thing, or even remember a singular event the same way. One thing I'm sure of is that when we contrive to make core memories with heavy investment in once-in-a-lifetime moments, we invariably end up remembering the smaller stuff around the edges instead. Knowing this, what kind of everyday joy do you want to pass on? Perhaps it's in the way you make yourself present for those around you, or in the simple steps you take to prepare a fun activity with someone else's enjoyment in mind. Or perhaps it's simply doing something you love for the people you love, every single day – something as easy and joyful as giving a hug.

The poet Mary Oliver was right when she wrote that 'Joy is not made to be a crumb', as if brushed off from someone else's plate. But the serving doesn't have to be big to fill you up if you taste it every day.

8

Aspiration

> '"Hope" is the thing with feathers – / That perches in the soul'
>
> Emily Dickinson, '"Hope" Is the Thing with Feathers'

THERE'S A ROOM RIGHT AT the back of the children's section of the National Museum of Denmark that's filled with doll's houses you can play with. I took my daughter there during the armpit of the year, the stretch between Christmas and New Year, when I was feeling fatigued from all the festivities and anxious about heading into another unknown year. My daughter was a moth to the flame, organizing furniture and reaching on her tiptoes so she could put the toilet in the en suite of some frothy mansion. That particular doll's house was the one that dominated her attention – four storeys of pink wonderland, unlike anything she'd ever seen before. I watched her play, oblivious to the other children around her, and felt a pang of nostalgia.

My body was in the room with my daughter but my mind had raced back thirty-plus years. I was reliving childhood playdates with an old school friend in her large family house, which had a dedicated playroom filled with costumes, craft materials, puzzles, games, an extensive array of My Little Pony models with fastidiously brushed hair, and so much more besides. But the pride of my friend's collection was the Barbie Dreamhouse, standing almost as tall as we were, filled with everything imaginable for all her well-attended dolls, including the hot-pink convertible in its garage. The whole thing was monstrously awesome, and I felt giddy looking at it. The thing is, I can't remember ever touching the Dreamhouse. I know I was allowed to, and my friend was constantly rearranging the rooms and sending her dolls out for trips in their car. But I just watched. I didn't want to play with the toy – I wanted the real thing. I wanted what the Dreamhouse represented.

As a kid, I was constantly daydreaming. Some of these scenarios were edits to events that had already happened, but most were wildly imagined futures. When many of us have a moment to ourselves at home, it's not uncommon to time-travel like this. We'll either remember things gone by or we'll daydream about what's to come. Both mental states promote the feeling of joy, which, as we learned in the previous chapter, is great for our overall health and well-being. Daydreaming about outlandish things is still something I like to do, but I've found that age has weakened the muscle. I have to work much harder to bring the images to mind now. Perhaps it's a tougher swing to get imaginative about a future that's invariably filled with fixed routines and certainty the older we get. This saddened me, to be honest. I like to think our future is always up to us, no matter how many candles are on the cake.

What is it that we're doing when we daydream about things to come? We're using the safe space of our mind to be hopeful about our future, even if the substance of it is beyond the realm of possibility. Some people call this 'thinking for pleasure', which brings to mind similar pursuits I talked about when exploring the benefits of nurturing in Chapter 6. Daydreaming is something that's well supported in a home environment – most particularly when a brace of our emotional needs have already been met, such as comfort and security. It's also easier to daydream when you know what brings you joy and have accomplishments to build on. All told, daydreams are particularly effective ways to flesh out our heart's desires. Which brings us to aspiration.

For a large chunk of my life, I would mostly daydream about external things – money, awards, marriage, beauty. Most often, the fantasies centred around living in one of those really big American houses I saw in every movie and TV show I watched. This kind of ephemera, the material gains of success, was what I aspired to for a long time. If you believe that energy flows where attention goes, then surely thinking purposely about these kinds of things – or 'manifesting' them, the currently trendy way of talking about it – is how we get them. And by some measure, I achieved a few of these things along the way. But it never felt enough. The metric would always move, the pool of comparison deepen. The dreams became less about hope and more about consolidating and benchmarking and never losing that foot in the door once it was there.

I'm not going to tell you what you should and shouldn't dream about for yourself, but in this chapter I want to share an idea that has turned my daydreams on their head. It's backed by research that shows intrinsic motivation is more powerful than extrinsic, and that people who channel their aspirations towards things like personal growth or deeper relationships report better well-being and overall life satisfaction. This is the basis of self-determination theory, and it has remarkable applications for life at home. In truth, it has made me totally re-evaluate the future of my own.

When we talk about aspiration in the context of the IKEA *Life at Home* research, we talk about feeling positive and prepared for our future. After a sense of accomplishment, aspiration presents the largest emotional gap, with a 38 per cent difference globally between expectation and reality. Of all the needs we have from the home, aspiration is the one that stretches my understanding of what an emotion is – can you *feel* aspiration? On this matter, I defer again to Brené Brown, who expanded on a whopping eighty-seven emotions and 'experiences' in her book *Atlas of the Heart*, explaining that experiences are 'thoughts which lead to emotion'. This is how aspiration finds us, then, as a series of thoughts – about ourselves and our future – which make us feel ready, resilient and optimistic for what's to come in our life at home.

Not everyone feels hopeful about their future. When we ask people their top concerns about their life at home, household finances and the general state of the economy tend to compete for the top spot, after physical and mental health, and our changing climate. The rising cost of living in a lot of countries has eaten into many people's hopes and dreams, with as many as one in ten people globally saying milestone events such as getting married and starting a family will be negatively affected. Perhaps this is why thinking for pleasure is harder than it seems. I was taken aback by a piece of research published in *Science* which revealed that many people don't like to be left with their thoughts. When the research participants were placed alone in a room for up to fifteen minutes, they reached for different forms of available stimuli to avoid having to think, including undertaking mundane tasks and giving themselves electric shocks. The research paper noted that 'many preferred to administer electric shocks to themselves instead of being left alone with their thoughts'. The research also showed that this was significantly more likely to happen for men than for women. It seems that spending time thinking positively about our future is not something that comes easily for most people, and it's getting even harder to reach in this increasingly frightening and overstimulated world of ours. So how can our homes help us out?

There are a few routes into aspiration, but they all work around a double-sided question:

- How can our home facilitate positive thoughts about our future?
- What kind of aspirations do we hold for our life at home?

We've walked a long path together through this book, and you might have noticed how the skills and solutions presented in earlier chapters help you build capacity for the emotional needs discussed in subsequent chapters. I like to think of the eight emotions working together to create exponential results, so that putting in place foundational needs like comfort and security leads to even greater returns when you come to connective needs like belonging and nurturing. This is why aspiration comes at the end – looking forwards, with hope and positivity, is far easier and more beneficial when everything else about life at home in the present feels good.

For the final time, I'll share my 'hands and heart' solutions to get us there. I'll bring into play some of the functional approaches I've already introduced, and I also want to push you on what it is you aspire towards. But before we get to that, I want to talk a little bit about our shared future. So many of our hopes and dreams, and the ways we need to prepare ourselves, are dependent on what happens in the world around us.

Aspiration is one part dreaming about the future, and one part feeling ready for it. Maybe that's why I like to use the word 'hopeful' when I talk about aspiration – because it feels like we have some skin in the game.

Most things ahead of us are easier to feel positive about if we've done all we can to prepare for them, no matter whether it's something we're excited about or that makes us anxious. Our home serves as a place to both dream and prepare, giving us a protected space for reflection alongside the ability to take action and surround ourselves with the cues we need to confirm that we're on our way.

As part of the *Life at Home* research for 2023, we looked into life at home in the present and we also did some dreaming about society's possible futures. That's futures in the plural, because there is no single, fixed future – there are many possibilities. We don't know exactly what will happen in the years ahead, of course, but we can make some reasonable guestimates based on a handful of certainties which track from events occurring today. And I'll be honest: it's not looking great. We'll continue to experience the impact of things like conflict, political and social polarization, financial crises, major health issues (including pandemics) and – certainly not least – rising global temperatures. Looking at the concerns that people say they have for the coming decade, published in the annual World Economic Forum's *Global Risk Perception Survey*, the ones about environmental risks – from extreme weather events to ecosystem collapse – dominate the top of the risk rankings, year on year.

Our changing climate is undeniable, and increasingly our day-to-day lives are grossly affected by the fallout. Home may provide a sanctuary, but we cannot escape reality – in fact, home is most likely where we find ourselves contemplating what our life will be like in a climate-changed future. For many people, the future is already here and their life at home has been devastated by major weather events, from wildfires to floods. It can be hard to stay positive or feel remotely prepared for circumstances which are enormous, interconnected and wildly complex. IKEA research into climate action shows that as many as seven in ten people globally say they worry about climate change, but almost as many say they take action against it daily. This is quietly reassuring. So, too, are the data from *Life at Home* research showing that 72 per cent of people who believe their home helps them live sustainably feel more positive about their life at home overall. My takeaway from this is that the road ahead is scary but we can afford to be more optimistic about the future when we're taking proactive steps today.

In the face of devastating climate-related events which quite literally destroy people's homes, it feels awfully glib to start talking about sustainable living as a lifestyle choice. And yet the rise of self-sufficiency, reducing our footprint, learning more trades and crafts, growing our own food – these are all things that have become aspirational for many people. This kind of future for life at home, one we have to work on with our hands and often through community, pulls in the other direction to the kind we're served up by tech entrepreneurs who promise us a life of unmitigated convenience and the end of flawed human interactions, thanks to frictionless AI. I get a lurching feeling in my stomach whenever I see those computer-generated images of glass pods and hovering cars we're supposed to be excited about taking over our cityscapes. Where did all the life go? As Nick Foster, one of the founders of Near Future Laboratory, put it in his brilliant essay 'The Future Mundane': 'Spaceships, weapons and computers are plentiful in science fiction cinema, but what about corkscrews, soccer cleats, milk packaging or garden hoses?'

Indeed, where is all the stuff of everyday life? When we conjured up a handful of different scenarios about home life ten years ahead, as part of the *Life at Home* research, we found ourselves on the side of positivity and preparedness. We also found ourselves in the everyday. What many of our fantasy families were doing in response to inevitable climate change in the future were the kinds of things we are already doing right now: eating more vegan and vegetarian meals, using renewable energy sources, fixing and swapping clothes and furniture, tending to the land and water around us. I know that sorting out the recycling might not feel, on the face of it, particularly aspirational for life at home, but doing these kinds of small and practical things makes all of us feel more positive about our shared future. That's the deepest meaning of aspiration.

If I'd asked you to tell me what you hope for in your future at the start of this chapter, I'm not sure you'd have talked about sustainability. Learning to live within the limits of the planet feels like retraction, rather than expansion, and no one wants to willingly put a cap on aspiration. Also, with the greatest of respect, eating vegan leftovers for the third night in a row is a chore, not a dream. Honestly, I'm not trying to bring the vibes down by talking about catastrophes and lentils; climate change frightens the hell out of me, but I have dreams too. I simply want to demonstrate that realizing aspiration – an essential ingredient in the feeling of home, let's not forget – is by its very nature dependent on what happens in our volatile world, not just the consequence of a really good imagination. I want us to take comfort in knowing that our aspiration knows no bounds when we connect it to something we're *all* invested in. When we want more for everyone, we get more for ourselves too.

Now that you know this, does it make you feel differently about your future?

Good. Then let's get into it.

A home for your future

When was the last time you had a proper daydream? I'd wager that in almost any circumstance where you find yourself killing time, you get your phone out. You see it everywhere outside the home: people hunched over personal devices whilst travelling, waiting for appointments, standing in queues, and so on. No time is too fleeting to see what other people are doing on the internet. But how about when you're inside your home?

If you've followed some of my solutions in Chapter 3, where we explored privacy in the context of security, you might have used some of that newly established alone-time to wander around your mind. It's possible, however, that you used it to wander around the internet – again. I'll take a punt and say that any recent thinking for pleasure has taken place whilst you've been busy doing other things – stacking the dishwasher, folding laundry, changing the bedsheets, unpacking the groceries, that kind of thing. It's easier to stay off your phone when your hands are engaged with other things, giving your mind the chance to wander.

Home is a great place to nurture your aspiration, not least because it's an ideal location to train yourself to think for pleasure. Later in this chapter we'll talk about *what* to focus on, but for now we're just getting into the *how*. You'll remember that in Chapter 3 we laid down some preconditions for privacy, and in Chapter 4 we zoned the home and took small actions to prime ourselves for accomplishment. Here, we'll revisit some of these techniques with the purpose of freeing our minds.

Let's start by reflecting on the spaces and opportunities where you are able to practise effective privacy. I want you to think about one location and / or one activity in your home which provides the most reliable context for letting your mind wander. This could be:

- Taking a shower
- Lying in bed before you fall asleep or when you wake up
- Watering your plants

- Preparing a meal
- Running the vacuum cleaner around your floors
- Sorting out the sock drawer

I want you to commit to using that golden opportunity to be with your thoughts at least three times a week. If you're like me, then that commitment will need some reinforcement against two irresistible distractions: your smartphone and the urge to mentally multitask.

Let's start with our phones. It's not just scrolling that's intrusive to thinking for pleasure, it's our tendency to use our phones for music, films and podcasts, too, all of which do a really effective job of filling the silence and keeping us entertained. Of course, there's a time and place for that, as we explored through nurturing and joy, but I want us all to protect some of our hard-won alone-time for thinking. I'm coming down hard on smartphones because they are consistently the worst offenders across a range of metrics, and they specifically interfere with things which enable us to think ahead and imagine goals for ourselves – like good sleep, being productive and better stress responses. What we're really dealing with here is addiction. Our handsets are not distracting per se, but we are using them to distract ourselves with microdoses of dopamine, which are immediately followed by a small crash.

As James Clear explains in his book *Atomic Habits*, which I discussed in Chapter 4, bad habits are hard to break because they are so easy and rewarding to do in the moment, even if they make us feel like garbage in the long run. Globally, people check their smartphones at least fifty-eight times a day on average, with 89 per cent of interactions initiated by the user rather than in response to a notification. We do that because we carry our phones on our person all the time, even when we're at home. The good news is that home is the best place to start severing that dependency, because we can leave our phone in a safe place and walk away from it.

When you make a commitment to be with your thoughts, try putting your phone in another location. Better yet, turn it off completely and, as I suggested in the previous chapter, shut it in a drawer or box for a fixed time. If the thought of being uncontactable for the duration of a daydream gives you acute anxiety (*What if this is the exact moment that my child breaks their neck at school – and the teacher cannot get hold of me?!*), then leave it on but know that you need to work even harder on the impulse to pick it up when it's not ringing. The best (and only) advice I have for this is to count to ten when you get the urge to check – it's just long enough to stop the instinct in its tracks, and makes you conscious of the habit you're trying to break.

With your phone out of sight and ideally out of mind, you can further work with your environment to support thinking for pleasure. As you might for your moments of privacy or nurturing rituals, prepare a comfy place to rest, consider noise reduction and introduce nice aromas, if you have the chance. Otherwise, doing something menial that requires very little complexity to complete, like folding sheets or washing dishes – something you might pick as a small shot of accomplishment – is a great way of occupying the hands to let the mind walk free. The irony is that you don't need to overthink what to do when you need to think. Keep it simple, so that you can move quickly and effortlessly into pondering.

With our environment in good shape, now we can talk about the other big distraction from daydreaming: mental multitasking. Personally speaking, I struggle with the idea of doing 'nothing', even if doing 'nothing' is still doing something, like sleeping or relaxing or daydreaming. Like many working parents, I head into each day with a never-ending list of things I have to do before the clock strikes midnight so I can wake up the next day and do it all again. Almost all of my scant downtime around the demands of my job and my family is used to multitask, so if I'm folding laundry then I'm also thinking about all the things that have to happen in the extremely near future, like making a shopping list, cleaning the bathroom and paying my bills. If I've got any more bandwidth after that, I'll venture on to things which will happen in the marginally-less-extremely-near future, like planning my daughter's birthday party, booking a dentist appointment and ordering new coats and shoes for children who refuse to stop growing. This is cognitive labour. Combining it with emotional labour – anticipating how people will feel and managing their emotions – is how we get to the 'mental load'. It is well documented that, generally, women carry more of the mental load than men, and mothers carry more of it than anyone.

The *Life at Home* research shows us that when you look at the difference between men and women and the things they say they find the most frustrating at home, women report all kinds of domestic chores whilst men are more likely to say things like 'not being able to do my hobbies' and 'not having a place to relax'. This point about frustration is important because the mental load is enormously taxing in and of itself, and it breeds resentment which chips away at our ability to frame our lives in a positive way. The mental load sucks the life out of daydreams and heavily encroaches on our potential to realize aspiration, because there is simply no time or positive capacity to reflect on what you want in the future when you have to remember to sign your kids up to swimming classes, buy more cat food, call the electrician, replace the bag in the vacuum cleaner, pick up a birthday present, bake a cake for the school summer fair, reply to your friends' messages and get that weird-looking mole checked out, all before lights out.

I'm sorry to say that I don't have a neat solution for hundreds of years of socialization around gendered activities at home or the fact that capitalist economies place no value on domestic work or child-rearing. I'm also sorry to say that when I offer any advice, at the moment it's a matter of 'Do as I say and not as I do' – I have been writing these words whilst my baby son naps, during which time I have also been simultaneously thinking about what to make my family for lunch, the ingredients we need for dinner, when to put the shelves up in the kids' room, what time the laundry will be finished, that the plants need watering and if my son is hitting all his milestones. In this season of my life I can barely focus on what I'm doing in the present, let alone in the future.

There is no silver bullet, but even in this current deluge of cognitive labour, there are three actions that help keep my thoughts on track which I can recommend:

→ **Talking**
With your partner, with your kids, with your flatmates – whoever coexists in your domestic space – and being proactive, honest and fair about what needs to be done and who needs to do it.

→ **Automating**
Meal plans, grocery orders, calendar reminders, bills and invoices . . . Make it automatic or schedule a specific time to do it so you don't think about it every waking minute of the day until you finally get around to it.

→ **Writing**
Getting something on paper means you don't have to hold it in your head. When I think about something I have to do and I'm in the middle of doing something else, I write it down on a small notepad by my desk. Then I can come back to it later.

There is one other simple idea worth trying, and that's making an aspiration talisman. It could be an object you always have on your person, or an item in your home imbued with meaning. I wear a locket on a necklace that makes me think about my family, and whenever I reach up to touch it I feel more positive and prepared for what's ahead. Recently I bought my husband a small Daruma doll, a traditional Japanese good-luck ornament, which sits on our bookshelf. The Daruma comes with two blank eyes – you colour in one when you make your wish, and the other one when the wish is fulfilled. Every time I look at that doll, when I'm tapping away on my laptop, I think about the aspirations we hold for ourselves and each other.

By making some proactive decisions about how you free up your headspace in your homespace, from locking your phone away to meal-planning for the week, it's possible to create the preconditions for positive, expansive and aspirational thinking about life at home. So now you have the time and mental space, what are you going to think about?

Before we travel to the future to find out, I want to briefly take you back in time.

A future for your home

When James and I moved to Copenhagen in 2015, it was with eyes firmly set on the future. We'd spent the previous year looking at increasingly desperate places to buy in far-flung suburbs of London, including one apartment, occupied by four students, that felt like it had been staged for an episode of *Punk'd*. There was black soot all the way up the kitchen walls and a fire-ravaged pan melted to the cooker hob, twenty (yes, twenty!) open packets of thrush cream on the bedroom floor and an almighty shit left floating in the toilet. The estate agent described it as a 'fixer-upper' but it was hard not to think that whatever had burst into flames in the kitchen had been put out too soon.

By the end, we'd started looking for properties so far out of London that the thought of moving to another country suddenly seemed quite reasonable. Once we'd set everything in motion for Denmark, we promised one another that we would do whatever it took to get on the property ladder over there. We wanted to find new jobs, get a cat, make friends, start a family. But what I really wanted – what I dreamed about – was a Big Home to put it all in.

Fast forward seven years, and things were going well. Jobs – check. Cat – check. Friends – check. Baby – check. We even did whatever it took and bought our first home, a small apartment two storeys up in a part of Copenhagen affectionately known as Shit Island, for reasons that have something to do with old municipal waste policies. Surely, then, the next step was moving on up.

I come from a culture that places a lot of emphasis on living in family-sized houses with enough bedrooms and toilets for everyone and a private back garden for al fresco lunches and kicking a ball around. After the meaningful encounter I shared in Chapter 1,

I'd put shame to one side and found comfort in raising our daughter in our cosy apartment. But as we contemplated having another child, I couldn't shake the idea that it was time to move to a Big Home. In a practical sense, I could cobble together a response to the question I asked myself repeatedly, usually at 2 a.m. during bouts of chronic insomnia: *Where will another baby go?* But I was struggling to answer it on an emotional level. This was the Barbie Dreamhouse all over again, three decades and twenty-five house-moves later.

Against the fraught backdrop of trying, failing and hoping for a second child, I wrestled with what it would mean to raise a family where we lived. And then some kind of cosmic magic occurred: we had a conditional offer accepted on a beautiful, family-sized house surrounded by a blossoming garden, at roughly the same time that I found out that I was pregnant. It was so precisely what I wanted, almost uncanny in the details I had dreamed of, that I could scarcely believe it. Perhaps that was the tell, because nothing went to plan.

The conditional offer on the house was contingent on selling our apartment, which, despite constant viewings, we just couldn't seem to do. Down one path I'd see two kids and a Big Home; down the other, life on hold. And then one Saturday in September, when I was three months pregnant – and just a day after a scan that showed a healthy heart, and perfect fingers and toes – I lost my baby. The following day, I helped tidy the apartment, bundled our cat into her box and bribed my toddler to put her shoes on so we could vacate for another unsuccessful viewing.

We shuffled on like this for another couple of months but as Christmas reared its head, James and I sat down and had a Proper Talk. We were exhausted, physically and emotionally. My mental health was shredded, and I wasn't doing anything which meaningfully nurtured me. We'd stopped experiencing joy, things felt entirely out of our control, and I was constantly plagued by what I thought of as the antithesis to accomplishment: stasis. In fact, all the important things that made life at home *feel like home* had started to fall away because we'd been so preoccupied with moving on. No wonder we were miserable. So, we took our home off the market. It was probably delayed grief, but I cried about it all weekend.

In early January, I went down to the local beach on my own. It was cold and quiet, just a few regular dog walkers zipped up in puffer jackets, nodding the occasional 'hello'. I sat by the water's edge with a sheet of paper and a pen, and I wrote down everything that was making me mad and sad. And then I wrapped the paper around a stone and threw it into the sea. If this was the movie of my life, the scene would cut away to me in reverent thought, but in reality the paper immediately came away from the stone and started to wash back up on to the shore, so I had to wade in to retrieve it, then put the paper in the bin instead. Sitting back down, with soggy feet, I made a pact with myself: *I will focus on the things I can do today which give me hope for tomorrow.*

This was the moment I started to draw on everything I had learned about life at home over the years. I got back to the essential truth – something I shared with you all the way back in Chapter 1 – that absolutely nothing has to change in your home for you to feel like it's a completely different place. In this way, I began to look inwards for motivation rather than outwards. I thought about what needed to happen for me to realize my dreams if the optics of my life remained the same. The Barbie Dreamhouse had all the proportions of aspiration, but it was just a plastic shell. Faced with my feelings during that chilly morning at the beach, it became clear that the dream of the Big Home was one of the things making me mad and sad. I wanted to feel hopeful about my life at home, and I wanted to be prepared for whatever might come. So, I got curious about the things that I could take action on today – things that were meaningful and satisfying in and of themselves, regardless of whether they led to an external goal. Softly, slowly, week by week, this was how I placed my dreams into the life I already had. This was how I found my way back home.

You'll have noticed that I have asked you many questions throughout this book, to help you expand on your understanding of yourself in the context of our emotional needs. If you have spent any time reflecting on them so far, then I'd say you're already well on your way to developing a more grounded and intrinsic approach to aspiration for your life at home. I'd now like to ask you some more, which are forged in the crucible of my own necessary and recent exploration.

They are designed to push you on a few 'hot button' areas as they relate to your life at home today and what you dream about for tomorrow.

All told, I've boiled the questions down to twelve provocations across four aspects of the home – the place our home is situated, the space we have around us, the people we live with and amongst, and things we bring into our home. I'd like to suggest that you have the following up your sleeve the next time you have a moment to think:

Place

- Does the balance of enjoyable time spent inside my home and outside it feel right?
- Do I actively put into my community what I expect to get out of it?
- Do I ask open questions about the way other people live, or am I making assumptions?

Space

- What would I do differently in my life if my home were a blank canvas, and what price – financial, physical, emotional – would I be willing to pay for it?
- What is something I ask other people to do for me at home that I could learn to do for myself?
- Do I lean into – or hold back from – a fulfilling creative life at home, and do I know what that means for me?

People

- Do I know what my 'love language' is at home, and do I speak it freely with the people I care about?
- Does my life at home today help or hinder me in being the kind of person (and, perhaps, parent) I strive to be?
- Do I show up for my friends the way I like them to show up for me?

Things

- Are my wants for my home also needs?
- Do the things I have around me reflect who I am, who I was, or who I want to be?
- If I lost all of my possessions tomorrow, which loss would I feel the most in five years' time?

I suspect you will gravitate towards some of these questions more than others, and some may not feel relevant for this season of your life. In other instances you may struggle to answer any of them at all. I know I did. Rest assured there is no test at the end, because there are no right or wrong answers. Please know that simply asking them is starting the work. Far too many of us plod on through a life built on absolutes and received wisdom. We just keep doing the things we have always done because they are expected of us, or we expect them of ourselves. Most often the consequence of responding to these provocations is a desire to make a change in our attitude or perspective. They help us prioritize things which are very seldom about social status or material possessions. We may find that we still deeply want for things – another baby, an extra bedroom, an easier commute – but now we know the value they hold in our lives, and not just the cost. My biggest hope for this part of your exploration is that you can shift fixed statements about your life and dreams into open questions.

You may notice that none of these questions directly address what we tend to call our 'life purpose'. They're not questions that ask you what it's all for and why you are uniquely positioned to do it. Elizabeth Gilbert, the bestselling author of numerous books, including *Eat, Pray, Love* and *Big Magic*, recently said that we're living through a period of 'purpose anxiety'. I agree. Many of us are so preoccupied with finding out what it is we're supposed to be doing with our lives that we overlook the fact we are already living them in so many good and meaningful ways, exactly where we already are. It can be a beautiful thing to know what your gifts are and give them freely to the world, but chasing down your purpose can become a distraction when it's decoupled from the matter of our daily domestic existence. I believe it is more than enough to show up today in a way that's good for you and the people around you, and feel hopeful for tomorrow. That's where these questions will take you. And if purpose comes knocking after all that, I know you'll be more than ready to honour it.

*

After that cold morning on the beach, fishing bits of paper out of the sea, I rode my bike through the quiet streets of Copenhagen, back home. I put the key in my front door with a new perspective. I had spent the previous year 'wintering', as Katherine May so evocatively describes the process of retreating inwards during times of loss and hardship. Now I was getting ready for my spring, with positivity and readiness for the future. And when the things I truly wanted came into my life in the following months and years, I was prepared to receive them.

When I reflect on the qualities of each of the eight emotional needs, I can't help but feel that aspiration is the one that comes out swinging when you call it. It's the steady hand when we need to be brave; the unwavering voice when we need a pep talk. Aspiration tells us to hope for the best while we get our literal and metaphorical house in order. Given the state of the world we're all facing, I believe that making where we live a place where we feel positive and prepared is the most aspirational thing any of us can do for our future.

CONCLUSION

A Never-ending Story

'When I get home, I shall write a book about this place. If I . . . If I ever do get home.'

Lewis Carroll, Alice in Wonderland

WHENEVER I SET OUT FROM home towards my local high street, I always look up to see the curling gilded spire of the Church of Our Saviour just a little further down the road. It's a magnificent piece of baroque architecture, most memorable for its four-hundred-step staircase which winds its way up from within the bowels of the church and finally spills out around the spire, like a corkscrew, to meet the golden orb at the tip. It looks like a huge whorl of bedazzled chocolate, straight out of a fairy tale, and it never fails to make me smile.

I've climbed those stairs a handful of times, mostly on days when Copenhagen is bathed in sunshine and the blue of the sky hits the blue of her waters and I think – as I often do – there is no place I would rather live. Whiteknuckled on the gold-painted handrail, I dare myself to look down at the roads, parks and canals, and then at the rooftops and windows of the homes spilling out far below me. Seen from above, the substance of these buildings suddenly shrinks to the simple matter of bricks, mortar, glass and steel. It's a helpful corrective on the days when I've let the expectation of home grow larger than the reality of my life.

I've been steeped in the topic of life at home for many years now, but writing about it for this book has frequently pushed my own experience of the subject to its limits. In many ways it became the book I needed to read, as I found myself confronted by fresh challenges to my emotional needs and frequently turning to the solutions I was proposing. Just as I was plotting my way through comfort and control, we welcomed another baby into our home and all the routines and rituals I had meaningfully placed into my life over the years came undone. Thinking of any kind, let alone for pleasure, was in short supply given that privacy was almost impossible to come by. My horizon for getting things done was abruptly pulled back from weeks and days to just hours and minutes. I became one of the millions of people who find themselves falling into the emotional gap, just as I had countless times before. The difference was that I saw it coming, and I knew how to get back out again.

This is how life at home goes. Some days home will make you feel great, and other days it'll make you feel mad and sad. Over the course of the previous eight chapters, I have set out each of the emotions we experience when we talk about 'feeling at home'. In some instances, I approached these emotions from the shadows as a way to illustrate what we're experiencing when we *don't* feel at home. I wanted to demonstrate that sometimes it's easier to see what we miss than what we possess. But I also wanted to demonstrate that life at home isn't always sunshine and roses, and invariably we have to take the salty with the sweet if we're sincere about having a meaningful and authentic life where we live.

The solutions I provided are tried-and-tested through my own scalding experiences of homemaking, and with thanks and gratitude to the many people I have met through the *Life at Home* research who shared their ways over the years. I hope that any one of these solutions helps you close an emotional gap where you find one. However, I want to emphasize that there's no set formula for getting it right. Whilst I'd like for you to have many of your needs met where you live – to feel at home as fully as possible – there will be different seasons of life when you need different things from your home. Moving away from your family, moving in with someone new, making commitments, having children, separation and divorce, getting pets, relocation, job loss, caretaking responsibilities, illness, retirement, grief, empty-nesting ... This constant expansion and contraction of your life will open and close various emotional gaps along the way. It's also likely that many of these events will take place under the same roof, given enough time. This is to remind you that the footprint of your home is not a proxy for the footprint of your life.

Just as there is no formula, there is no formal hierarchy or pyramid for the needs, either. I presented them in a chronology that reaches from the everyday to the future, because this sequence feels the most applicable to how we frequently interact with our homes and what we ask of them. In our daily touch-points with home, we need to feel secure, comfortable and in control of the space around us. Then we reach for accomplishment, because living is forward momentum, just as we continually deepen the connection with ourselves and the people around us. We come to joy through pleasure and intention, and then we may turn our minds – and our hearts – to hopes and dreams ahead. There is a certain exponential energy when we follow the needs in this way, and I believe that it's easier to find subsequent needs like belonging and joy when our daily essentials are taken care of. However, I know that many of us – me included – have lived in places which shortchanged us on the basics, and we still found the resilience and hope to aspire for a better life at home. In any kind of combination or sequence, the eight emotional needs hold equal weight as we balance life with where we live. When our relationship with home is built on an honest understanding of how it feels to live there and what it takes to make it better, then I believe it can withstand the pendulum-swing. I believe *you* can withstand the pendulum-swing. The trick is to be in mindful attendance, just as you would with any other important relationship in your life. You now have the knowledge to do exactly that.

Furthermore, this means that, unlike a kitchen renovation or an attic extension, there is no completion date for a better life at home. There's no fixed point when you can step back, dust off your hands and head to the pub after a job well done. There is only the organic, pulsing heart of your home in any single moment, on any single day. Perhaps this is a little overwhelming to contemplate, particularly if you have been socialized to believe in the 'Forever Home'. It's OK, I understand. I'm not trying to stop us from striving for good, or holding on to something that might feel stable and permanent when so much else is in constant motion. I just want to liberate us all from the tyranny of a domestic finish line. Life at home is for living, not for winning and putting on a mantle.

The more I think about it, the more I feel that the idea of the Forever Home has done us dirty. It's up there with Happily Ever After in romantic relationships – the stuff of fairy tales. Forever Homes are synonymous with 'dream' and 'perfect' homes, implying that if your current home is neither of these things, then it's just somewhere you're passing through. And if you're just passing through, then you stop paying attention to the way it makes you feel. It reminds me of a memorable home visit in the early days of the *Life at Home* research, when we met a young man who had moved to England five years earlier. The apartment he was living in was 'just temporary', he told us, although it was the place he'd been living in since he'd first arrived in the country. He talked about wanting to find a 'Forever Family Home', a place he would lovingly decorate and renovate, finding space for all his cherished things and the theoretical children he would have. In the meantime, all the stuff he acquired was dumped behind the sofa in the living room, out of sight. As time went by, the sofa was nudged further and further into the room as the pile of stuff behind it grew and grew, until the space around the sofa became barely usable. Just before the home visit started, in a fit of desperation, he threw a huge rug over it all because he felt so ashamed. 'Just temporary' is an awfully long time to live anywhere that doesn't feel like home. What's more, there's simply no guarantee that finding and perfecting the Forever Home of your dreams, the one with the huge open kitchen and Moroccan-tiled wet room, is going to deliver on all your emotional needs. Even people in fairy tales must contend with the dishes and the laundry, and with navigating the kinds of love and loss that being part of families and communities involves.

I hope that reading about my own many and varied homemaking experiences has encouraged you to reflect on yours. You may find that this kind of thinking starts to pull a red thread through your life where previously you saw no connection between different homes. As someone who lives in a country where I was neither born nor raised, I often get asked by well-intentioned Danes where I 'come from'. To be clear, it is a privilege, as a white woman, to be asked that question from the perspective of someone just trying to land my accent, and not for more egregious reasons that relate to skin colour. I find it such an unimaginative question, with no simple answer. Is the inquisitor looking for a country, a city, a street? Do they want to know where I was born or where I was raised or where I have spent the most time? I have found that the story of where I come from is actually about where I have *be*come from, and this is a multifaceted thing. Who we become is tightly bound up with where we have lived. You cannot unpack the person you are today from all the different places and spaces you've called home along the way, much like you cannot remove the eggs or butter from a cake. This also leaves so much glorious potential ahead of us, rather than feeling that the mere circumstance of our birth-nationality leaves us frozen in existence. It makes me think of this glorious line from Colson Whitehead's *The Colossus of New York*: 'Cherish your old apartments and pause for a moment when you pass them. Pay tribute, for they are the caretakers for your reinventions.' How liberating to know that there are so many more places where we will continue to become ourselves, not least the constantly evolving nature of just one place – home.

Where do you become from? How much of yourself do you find at home? Do you feel at home where you live, or do you reach into other spaces and places to make up the deficit? I hope this book has helped you answer these important questions, and many more besides. When I was crying on the bus every day, coming back from my Microsoft Excel beginner's course in that wilderness period of my life before Paul saved me, my father sat me down in his studio and lovingly reminded me that things can change in a day. There is just the setting sun and the rising moon between the life you're living today, and the life you might live tomorrow. He was right, of course. Almost everything that changes in our life, good or bad, feels like it comes all at once. A decision. An action. A consequence. I take this to mean that I can create change of my own with nothing more than the freedom of twenty-four hours ahead of me. And that, as I hope I've demonstrated through research and time-worn experience, home is the biggest change-maker in our lives. The way we feel about home has a direct impact on how we feel about ourselves. So, when we make a change at home, whether that's removing shame and powerlessness or creating more privacy, joy and belonging, we're taking the opportunity to change our entire outlook on life.

Now that we've finished this journey home together, you may find yourself at the start of a new one. I hope you take this book as your loving companion along the way. A friend once told me that the things we learn about ourselves from our past experiences and behaviours open little windows and doors into our heart, and we get to choose whether we just take a look or step inside. It's a beautiful way of reflecting on how we process all the stuff that comes out when we start digging around. In a therapeutic sense, the heart is where we find our Forever Home. It's the place within us that we can retreat to, again and again, when life asks enormous things which often feel unanswerable and we reach for something that has been so hard to explain for so long, until now – the feeling of home.

I am more certain than ever that we all deserve to feel at home, no matter where we live. We *need* to feel at home. It's where the heart is.

Acknowledgements

My first thanks go to IKEA and its many talented and passionate people, who champion the importance of a better life at home. I am deeply indebted to David Affentranger, who brought me into the fold and gave me the extraordinary opportunity to lead the IKEA *Life at Home* Report back in 2017. My thanks also to Belén Frau Uriarte, who understood the potential of this topic and my desire to write a book about it all. Further thanks to Matias Bergknut, Steven Whyte and Fredrik Bengtsson, who all helped ensure I got the runway I needed in big ways and small.

The IKEA *Life at Home* Report has many midwives – far too many to list in full here – but I want to give special thanks to Maria Jonsson and Maria Jeansson, who helm the research behind the report and have been outstanding collaborators. Many thanks to my 'half walnut' Annika Mohlin, who worked in lockstep with me on the report in its early years. My thanks and appreciation go to all the IKEA country leaders who have invited me around the world, from Lisbon to Guangzhou, to run workshops and speak on the topic of life at home. A very grateful thanks to Ben Hayman and the whole team at Given Agency, who have been long-standing partners on the report. And, of course, none of this would have been possible without the many people who invited IKEA into their homes and took part in the research. Thank you for all the amazing home visits and for sharing your stories.

I'm deeply grateful to my agent Gordon Wise at Curtis Brown who, along with Elliot Prior, immediately understood what I wanted to do with this book and found it a home. It has been a joy collaborating with my editor Lucy Oates at Transworld, and I am indebted to her expertise and thoughtful input throughout the drafting process and beyond. Many thanks also to Megan Staunton at Bergstrom Studio, who saw the potential of my early proposal and helped get it over the line.

One of the reasons I feel so at home in Copenhagen is because of the friends I've come to know and love since we moved here. In particular, I want to thank Luka Whiteley – my very first friend in this city – who has extended much kindness and continues to inspire me with their exploration around identity. My love and thanks to Lucy Taylor-Gee, who has walked along much of the same path as I have and continues to show me the way whenever I am feeling lost. I'd be further marooned without Monica Keaney, who understands everything I mean even when I can't string a whole sentence together. My love and thanks also to Sherilyn Hellberg, who knows just what it takes to write a book and has been an outstanding cheerleader for mine. My gratitude to Nina Vlemmings, who has opened her home – and her heart – to me countless times. A special thanks to Kate Poulsson Johnson, who said something very wise to me many years ago that helped bring the threads of my book together at the end. Thank you – all of you – for opening up about your own lives at home with me, and for all the support and laughter whilst I've been writing this book. Further thanks to Alex and Martin Beck, who generously let me borrow their new studio space (and quickly painted it and installed lights) so I could knuckle down with the manuscript just before my deadline. A big thanks also to Lauren Chaney Sorensen and all the members of *The Ladies' Run & Dip Club*, who show up no matter the weather, fair or foul. I'll see you out there next Wednesday.

If I have a home from home when I am away from Copenhagen, then it is in the company of my oldest friends. My love and thanks to Jennifer Blainey, who met me underground when we were both in period costume and has kept me real ever since. And the same to Joanna Kennedy and Kate Cowcher, who regularly inspire me by demonstrating, in thought and deed, how to be brave, brilliant and curious. All my love to Tash Walker, who has known me the very longest and understands the origin story for it all.

I am indebted to my parents, Moy McCrory and Bob Moulder, who taught me the power of storytelling and provided much of the substance on which I have built a meaningful life at home – along with the ability to write about it. And I am so grateful for the love and friendship of my sister, Sorcha McCrory, who makes my life all the richer. But when all is said and done, I reserve the deepest of my love and gratitude for James Clasper – my gentle husband and co-parent – who has held my hand through thick and thin, and provided his significant skills and talent to help polish every stone in the editing of this book; and for our two incredible children, Órla and Rufus, who make it all worthwhile.

Resources

It won't be surprising to hear that the majority of the data and insights featured in this book are from the IKEA *Life at Home* Report, given this work is the touchstone of my approach to exploring a better life at home. The IKEA *Life at Home* Report has been published annually since 2014, and you can find all the reports available for download in the 'Past reports' section of the dedicated *Life at Home* website: https://lifeathome.ikea.com

Below, I share some more details about the people, organizations and materials which have informed my approach. Specific citations for data, insights and quotes that I've referenced throughout the book come in the Endnotes section.

INTRODUCTION

Professor Alison Blunt is the founding co-director of the Centre for Studies of Home, an interdisciplinary research hub jointly run by Queen Mary University of London and the Museum of the Home. You can read more about their work here: https://www.centreforstudiesofhome.org.uk. I met Professor Blunt during the development of the IKEA *Life at Home* Report 2018, and you can read more about her influence and involvement in our research in that report.

My approach to this book has also been inspired by the work of Michelle Ogundehin, whom I've had the pleasure of working with a few times over the years in relation to different editions of the IKEA *Life at Home* Report. Michelle is the former editor-in-chief of the British *ELLE Decoration* magazine, a presenter of the popular TV show *Interior Design Masters* and a kindred spirit in her views on the power of home to create better health and well-being. I thoroughly recommend her book *Happy Inside: How to Harness the Power of Home for Health and Happiness* (Ebury Publishing, 2020).

CHAPTER 1: COMFORT

In this chapter, I reference the work of the renowned researcher and storyteller Brené Brown. If Brown's work is new to you, please do check out her website first: https://brenebrown.com. Brené Brown is a prolific author, speaker and podcaster, and her wisdom is shared across it all. Several of her books were deeply informative as I approached the complex relationship between comfort and shame, namely *Daring Greatly: How the Courage to Be Vulnerable Transforms the Way We Live, Love, Parent and Lead* (Avery, 2015), *The Gifts of Imperfection* (Ebury Publishing, 2020) and *Atlas of the Heart: Mapping Meaningful Connection and the Language of Human Experience* (Ebury Publishing, 2021). Brown's podcast, *Unlocking Us*, is a great listen, and it's also worth going back to her viral 2010 TEDxHouston talk on vulnerability, https://www.ted.com/talks/brene_brown_the_power_of_vulnerability, and the follow-up she did on shame in 2012, https://www.ted.com/talks/brene_brown_listening_to_shame

If you're interested in reading more about the happiness rankings of different countries around the world, head to https://worldhappiness.report. The most recent ranking placed Denmark second in the world. There's always something to strive for!

CHAPTER 2: CONTROL

In this chapter, I reference the work and expertise of psychotherapist Esther Perel. If Perel's work is new to you, I recommend checking out her website: https://www.estherperel.com. Perel is a profoundly insightful and original voice on modern relationships, and freely shares a lot of her wisdom (and fantastic writing) on her website and through her regular newsletter 'Letters from Esther'. Perel is also the host of the popular podcast *Where Should We Begin?*, which provides an intimate glimpse into relationships between real couples. Furthermore, she has a number of highly viewed TED talks, in addition to an online TED Salon event during the pandemic where she talked about the importance of routines, rituals and boundaries – themes I touch on in subsequent chapters – at https://www.ted.com/talks/esther_perel_the_routines_rituals_and_boundaries_we_need_in_stressful_times?subtitle=en

I also touch on the subject of renting in relation to the data and insights which are included in the IKEA *Life at Home* Report and my own experiences. For an extensive and compelling look into the challenges within the rental market in the UK specifically, I recommend *Tenants: The People on the Frontline of Britain's Housing Emergency* by Vicky Spratt (Profile Books, 2023). I also found *Estates: An Intimate History* by Lynsey Hanley (Granta Books, 2023) a very moving read on the connected topics of homeownership and social housing.

CHAPTER 3: SECURITY

This chapter explores the feeling of security through the context of privacy, and a good deal of the data and insights I've referenced relating to this topic are from the IKEA *Life at Home* Report 2019, which was subtitled *The Power of Privacy*. If you only read one of these reports in full, I feel that this one might get you thinking the most.

I briefly mention the work of Dr Becky Kennedy in the context of how to talk to children about privacy and establish boundaries. Dr Becky (as she likes to be known) is a clinical psychologist and the author of the enormously popular book *Good Inside: A Practical Guide to Becoming the Parent You Want to Be* (HarperCollins, 2022). You can read more about her approach in helping families develop great relationships here: https://www.goodinside.com. If you're interested in further literature about parenting (and being parented), I also highly recommend *The Book You Wish Your Parents Had Read (and Your Children Will Be Glad That You Did)* by Philippa Perry (Penguin Books, 2020) and *The Daily Dad: 366 Meditations on Parenting, Love and Raising Great Kids* by Ryan Holiday (Profile Books, 2023).

CHAPTER 4: ACCOMPLISHMENT

In this chapter, I reference the work of James Clear and his popular concept of 'atomic habits'. If you're not familiar with Clear's work, I recommend checking out his website first: https://jamesclear.com. At various points in the chapter, I quote Clear from his bestselling book *Atomic Habits: An Easy & Proven Way to Build Good Habits & Break Bad Ones* (Random House Business Books, 2018), and I thoroughly recommend reading this insightful and instructional book in full for a deep immersion in his approach.

Other books which have influenced my approach include: *Deep Work: Rules for Focused Success in a Distracted World* by Cal Newport (Grand Central Publishing, 2016); *Happiness by Design: Finding Pleasure and Purpose in Everyday Life* by Paul Dolan (Penguin Books, 2014); *Bird by Bird: Some Instructions on Writing and Life* by Anne Lamott (Anchor Books, 1995); and *The Writing Life* by Annie Dillard (Harper Perennial, 1990).

CHAPTER 5: BELONGING

I'm not sure I've read another book quite as stealthy in capturing my heart as *The Colossus of New York* by Colson Whitehead (Doubleday, 2003). It is a perfect distillation of what it feels like to belong to a place and, given my deep love and affection for that certain place in particular, I hold it very close.

Many other writers have approached the way that geography and place interact with identity and belonging – far too many to mention here – but a few notable books that have influenced my thinking include: *A Field Guide to Getting Lost* (Canongate Books, 2017) and *The Faraway Nearby* (Granta Books, 2022), both by Rebecca Solnit; *Living Autobiography* by Deborah Levy, specifically the second volume, *The Cost of Living* (Penguin Books, 2019), and *Real Estate* (Penguin Books, 2022); *Places of the Heart: The Psychogeography of Everyday Life* by Colin Ellard (Bellevue Literary Press, 2015); and *Geography of Home* by Akiko Busch (Princeton Architectural Press, 1999).

If you're interested in learning more about the creative work of the Özçetin sisters, head to https://www.hamide.dk. They still sell the T-shirts.

CHAPTER 6: NURTURING

I first read *Wintering: The Power of Rest and Retreat in Difficult Times* by Katherine May (Ebury Press, 2020) during a long and cold winter of my own. It put me back in touch with my own need for nurturing, and also gave me the impetus I needed to write this book. I can also highly recommend May's follow-up book, *Enchantment: Reawakening Wonder in an Exhausted Age* (Faber & Faber, 2023), which addresses our innate need for wonder and awe. Katherine May also has a great podcast called *How We Live Now*.

In this chapter, I mention the power of asking yourself 'why'. The master of this is, of course, Simon Sinek, who wrote the book *Start with Why* (Penguin Books, 2011). I still think his viral 2009 TEDxPugetSound talk is a perfect example of how to drive your message home: https://www.youtube.com/watch?v=u4ZoJKF_VuA

CHAPTER 7: JOY

Apparently, the patron saint of joy is St Philip Neri, but if I were to pick a contemporary (and living) one, it would possibly have to be Meik Wiking. In this chapter, I reference one of Wiking's books, *The Art of Making Memories: How to Create and Remember Happy Moments* (Penguin Life, 2019), but I was also inspired by his other books, including *My Hygge Home: How to Make Home Your Happy Place* (Penguin Books, 2022) and, of course, his OG work, *The Little Book of Hygge: The Danish Way to Live Well* (Penguin Books, 2016). You can find more of Meik Wiking's work at The Happiness Research Institute: https://www.happinessresearchinstitute.com or visit The Happiness Museum if you are in Copenhagen.

When it comes to play, IKEA has released four *Play* Reports to date. You can find the 2024 edition here: https://www.ikea.com/global/en/our-business/reports/play-report-2024-240611/

In my research about joy, I also discovered this fun NPR Joy Generator, https://apps.npr.org/joy-generator, which is a lovely way of being (even more) playful with the good stuff.

CHAPTER 8: ASPIRATION

Some of the topics I touch on in this chapter are big and meaty ones: climate change, gender equality, self-determination theory. I have been inspired by many writers and thinkers as I've explored these issues from the vantage point of my own life at home, but I wanted to reference a few in particular here.

I'd like to start by saying that it can be easy to feel overwhelmed by the scale of things going horribly wrong around the world, and if you find yourself in need of a steadying hand then I can recommend *Factfulness: Ten Reasons We're Wrong About the World – And Why Things Are Better Than You Think* by Hans Rosling (Sceptre, 2018). I also had the pleasure of speaking on a panel discussion with Anna Rosling Rönnlund, from Gapminder, who invented *Dollar Street* – a brilliant and interactive website designed to provide visual information about life at home for people across all kinds of income levels around the world. It busts a lot of myths and demonstrates that we all have more in common than we assume: https://www.gapminder.org/dollar-street?

When talking about the future of life at home, I quoted from an excellent essay called 'The Future Mundane' by Nick Foster. You can read the full essay here: https://www.core77.com/posts/25678/the-future-mundane-25678. Nick is one of the founders of a think-and-do-tank called Near Future Laboratory, along with Julian Bleecker, who I collaborated with on a piece of design fiction for the very first IKEA *Life at Home* magazine. If the concept of 'design fiction' is new to you (as it was to me, before I met Nick), I can highly recommend tracking down a copy of *The Manual of Design Fiction* by Julian Bleecker, Nick Foster, Fabien Girardin and Nicolas Nova (Near Future Laboratory, 2022). This kind of thinking gets me excited about what lies ahead.

In this chapter, I mentioned my miscarriage. During that time, my sister gave me two books which I found deeply helpful in understanding what kind of shape grief can take in your life, namely Joan Didion's *The Year of Magical Thinking* (Fourth Estate, 2005) and a newly released version of *A Grief Observed – Readers' Edition* by C. S. Lewis (Faber & Faber, 2015). There is no right way to grieve any kind of loss – only your way.

When it comes to asking the important questions, I've found many depths in *Becoming Wise: An Inquiry into the Mystery and Art of Living* by Krista Tippett (Penguin Press, 2016), as well as all kinds of excellence in Cheryl Strayed's *Tiny Beautiful Things: Advice on Love and Life from Dear Sugar* (Atlantic Books, 2012). I mention Elizabeth Gilbert in relation to her views on 'purpose anxiety', and it would be fair to say that her book *Big Magic: Creative Living Beyond Fear* (Bloomsbury, 2015) had a profound effect on me, as I know it has on many other people. But if there's one person who's asked – and answered – the hardest questions, I'd say it's Nora Ephron. Her (republished) collection of essays, *I Feel Bad About My Neck: And Other Thoughts on Being a Woman* (Transworld, 2020), is a masterclass in form.

Endnotes

INTRODUCTION

1   1   'Home is a place we all must find': *The Wiz*, film directed by Sidney Lumet, Universal Pictures and Motown Productions (1978)

7   one in three people globally: IKEA *Life at Home* Report 2018 (Ingka Holding B.V.)

7   on top of household chores: IKEA *Life at Home* Report 2023 (Ingka Holding B.V.)

7   sleep as a way to relax: ibid.

7   watching their pets sleep: ibid.

10   home was their sanctuary: IKEA *Life at Home* Report 2020 (Ingka Holding B.V.)

10   made changes to their home: IKEA *Life at Home* Report 2021 (Ingka Holding B.V.)

10   At the heart of these insights: IKEA *Life at Home* Report 2022 (Ingka Holding B.V.)

10   they don't feel a sense of belonging: ibid.

13   'the quality of our relationships': Esther Perel, https://www.estherperel.com (accessed 16 November 2024)

CHAPTER 1: COMFORT

15   'There is nothing like staying at home': Jane Austen, *Emma* (John Murray, 1816)

17 they seldom get it: IKEA *Life at Home* Report 2023 (Ingka Holding B.V.)

17 regularly reflected in the media: IKEA *Life at Home* Report 2022 (Ingka Holding B.V.)

19 Brown defines shame: Brené Brown, *The Gifts of Imperfection* (Ebury Publishing, 2020)

23 'We're all afraid of shame': ibid.

24 'let our true selves be seen': ibid.

26 'We feel exhausted': ibid.

39 clutch of associated feelings: ibid.

CHAPTER 2: CONTROL

43 'people give up their power': Alice Walker, no date

43 'our sense of agency': Esther Perel and Mary Alice Miller, 'Letters from Esther #43: "Would you rather be right or be married?"', estherperel.com, https://www.estherperel.com/blog/letters-from-esther-42-would-you-rather-be-right-or-be-married

45 'priced accommodation': Danmarks Nationalbank, 'Market Concentration and the Danish Rental Market', 22 April 2022, https://www.nationalbanken.dk/media/33dlm50f/economic-memo-nr-5-2022.pdf (accessed 18 November 2024)

46 70 per cent own their home: 'House or flat – owning or renting', Eurostat, https://ec.europa.eu/eurostat/cache/digpub/housing/bloc-1a.html (accessed 18 November 2024)

46 28 per cent on average seldom experience it: IKEA *Life at Home* Report 2023 (Ingka Holding B.V.)

48 too much clutter: IKEA *Life at Home* Report 2022 (Ingka Holding B.V.)

48 less likely to experience enjoyment: ibid.

- 48 mental health improved: IKEA *Life at Home* Report 2021 (Ingka Holding B.V.)
- 51 'the need for control': Lauren A. Leotti, Sheena S. Iyengar and Kevin N. Ochsner, 'Born to choose: the origins and value of the need for control', *Trends in Cognitive Sciences*, 14: 10 (2010), pp. 457–63, https://www.ncbi.nlm.nih.gov/pmc/articles/PMC2944661/ (accessed 16 November 2024)
- 54 people have spoken to their plants: IKEA *Life at Home* Report 2022 (Ingka Holding B.V.)
- 56 'Make the best of what is in our power': 'Who is Epictetus? From slave to world's most sought after philosopher', Daily Stoic, https://dailystoic.com/epictetus/ (accessed 18 November 2024)
- 57 liberate us from defeating narratives: Esther Perel, 'Letters from Esther #23: Stories', https://www.estherperel.com/blog/letters-from-esther-23-stories (accessed 16 November 2024)
- 66 'Life throws you curveballs': IKEA *Life at Home* Report 2017 (Ingka Holding B.V.)
- 66 people with 'drive': ibid.

CHAPTER 3: SECURITY

- 68 'The ache for home': Maya Angelou, *All God's Children Need Travelling Shoes* (Random House, 1986)
- 68 bars on the windows: IKEA *Life at Home* Report 2023 (Ingka Holding B.V.)
- 69 during the pandemic: IKEA *Life at Home* Report 2020 (Ingka Holding B.V.)
- 70 top three needs: IKEA *Life at Home* Report 2023 (Ingka Holding B.V.)

- 70 home provides enough privacy: IKEA *Life at Home* Report 2022 (Ingka Holding B.V.)
- 70 someone will take it personally: IKEA *Life at Home* Report 2019 (Ingka Holding B.V.)
- 71 hidden from their housemates: IKEA *Life at Home* Report 2022 (Ingka Holding B.V.)
- 74 activities that enable personal growth: IKEA *Life at Home* Report 2019 (Ingka Holding B.V.)
- 76 don't have enough money: ibid.
- 76 shut a door to achieve privacy: ibid.
- 77 number one barrier to privacy: ibid.
- 78 Parents of young children: ibid.
- 78 likely to look at their phones: ibid.
- 78 Non-verbal actions: ibid.
- 79 the lowest of all the options: ibid.
- 79 women who say they feel frustrated: ibid.
- 84 privacy as-and-when: ibid.
- 89 outdoors in nature: ibid.
- 89 privacy at home: ibid.
- 91 fundamental to their well-being: ibid.

CHAPTER 4: ACCOMPLISHMENT

- 95 'To be yourself': *Ralph Waldo Emerson: Essays* (A Word to the Wise, 2014)
- 97 accomplishment has the biggest emotional gap: IKEA *Life at Home* Report 2023 (Ingka Holding B.V.)
- 99 tap into more accomplishment: ibid.
- 99 increased mental health concerns: IKEA *Life at Home* Report 2021 (Ingka Holding B.V.)

100 'depends on the quality of our habits': James Clear, *Atomic Habits* (Cornerstone, 2018)

101 'the victim of your environment': ibid.

109 'where there are pretty things': L. M. Montgomery, *Anne of Green Gables* (L. C. Page & Co., 1908)

110 'It will give you a small sense of pride': Admiral William H. McRaven, University of Texas at Austin 2014 Commencement Address, https://www.youtube.com/watch?v=pxBQLFLei70 (accessed 16 November, 2024)

118 'Just take it bird by bird': Anne Lamott, *Bird by Bird* (Anchor Books, 1995)

120 '"See where I have been led."' Henry Ford, no date

CHAPTER 5: BELONGING

121 'something of yourself': Fred Rogers, *Mr Rogers' Neighborhood* (WQED Studios, no date)

122 'our horizon of possibility shrinks': Geoffrey L. Cohen, *Belonging: The Science of Creating Connection and Bridging Divides* (W. W. Norton & Company, 2022)

123 disconnected or misunderstood: IKEA *Life at Home* Report 2023 (Ingka Holding B.V.)

124 wanting to go solo: IKEA *Life at Home* Report 2022 (Ingka Holding B.V.)

127 'accepted for being who you are': Brené Brown, *Atlas of the Heart* (Ebury Publishing, 2021)

129 sense of neighbourly belonging: IKEA *Life at Home* Report 2021 (Ingka Holding B.V.)

130 didn't know *any* of their neighbours: Leslie Davis and Kim Parker, 'A half-century after "Mister Rogers" debut, 5 facts about neighbors in U.S.', Pew Research Centre, August 15 2019, https://www.pewresearch.org/

short-reads/2019/08/15/facts-about-neighbors-in-u-s/ (accessed 16 November 2024)

130 chatting with a neighbour: IKEA *Life at Home* Report 2023 (Ingka Holding B.V.)

138 home doesn't show who they are: IKEA *Life at Home* Report 2022 (Ingka Holding B.V.)

140 best things about being together: IKEA *Life at Home* Report 2023 (Ingka Holding B.V.)

141 'one glance at a private space': Malcolm Gladwell, *Blink: The Power of Thinking Without Thinking* (Little, Brown and Company, 2005)

141 One in twenty people admitted as much: IKEA *Life at Home* Report 2022 (Ingka Holding B.V.)

142 the homes of their friends: ibid.

150 'New York will go on without us': Colson Whitehead, *The Colossus of New York* (Doubleday, 2003)

CHAPTER 6: NURTURING

152 'Seek home for rest': Thomas Tusser, *Five Hundred Points of Good Husbandry* (1573)

152 a reflection of themselves: IKEA *Life at Home* Report 2022 (Ingka Holding B.V.)

154 'letting your spare time expand': Katherine May, *Wintering: The Power of Rest and Retreat in Difficult Times* (Ebury Press, 2020)

155 unwind and relax: IKEA *Life at Home* Report 2023 (Ingka Holding B.V.)

155 more important amongst older people: ibid.

155 these two actions as rituals: IKEA *Life at Home* Report 2021 (Ingka Holding B.V.)

156 1.4 billion guests: 'Airbnb announces first quarter 2023 results', 9 May 2023, https://airbnb2020ipo.q4web.com/press-releases/news-details/2023/Airbnb-Announces-First-Quarter-2023-Results/ (accessed 16 November 2024)

164 completion of domestic chores: IKEA *Life at Home Report 2023* (Ingka Holding B.V.)

166 'demonstrated greater authenticity': Güler Boyraz, J. Brandon Waits and Victoria A. Felix, 'Authenticity, life satisfaction, and distress: a longitudinal analysis', *Journal of Counseling Psychology*, 61: 3 (2014), pp. 498–505, https://www.researchgate.net/publication/263896022_Authenticity_Life_Satisfaction_and_Distress_A_Longitudinal_Analysis (accessed 16 November 2024)

166 hobbies or personal projects: IKEA *Life at Home Report 2021* (Ingka Holding B.V.)

169 likely to prioritize self-care: ibid.

175 'Mealtime was more influential': Bruce Feiler, *The Secrets of Happy Families: Improve Your Mornings, Rethink Family Dinner, Fight Smarter, Go Out and Play – and Much More* (William Morrow, 2013)

CHAPTER 7: JOY

177 'Joy is not made to be a crumb': Mary Oliver, *Devotions: The Selected Poems of Mary Oliver* (Penguin Press, 2017)

178 experiencing joy: Mark Holder, 'Happiness and Your Immune System', *Psychology Today*, 9 June 2017, https://www.psychologytoday.com/us/blog/the-happiness-doctor/201706/happiness-and-your-immune-system (accessed 16 November, 2024)

178 help pain management: Rachel Müller, Alexandra L. Terrill, Mark P. Jensen et al., 'Happiness, pain intensity, pain interference, and distress in individuals with physical disabilities', *American Journal of Physical Medicine & Rehabilitation*, 94: 12 (2015), https://pubmed.ncbi.nlm.nih.gov/25802959/ (accessed 16 November, 2024)

178 increase our lifespan: Helen Fields, 'Happiness associated with longer life', *Science*, 31 October 2011, https://www.science.org/content/article/happiness-associated-longer-life (accessed 16 November 2024)

179 deficit of domestic joy: IKEA *Life at Home* Report 2022 (Ingka Holding B.V.)

179 'happiness is a solid': J. D. Salinger, 'De Daumier-Smith's Blue Period', *Nine Stories* (Little, Brown and Company, 1953)

182 hugs with a loved one: IKEA *Life at Home* Report 2023 (Ingka Holding B.V.)

187 play is actually a mindset: IKEA *Play* Report 2017, https://www.ingka.com/wp-content/uploads/2020/01/IKEA-Play-Report-2017.pdf

190 where things live around the home: IKEA *Life at Home* Report 2022 (Ingka Holding B.V.)

193 doing domestic chores: ibid.

194 'waiting for the other shoe to drop': Brené Brown, *Daring Greatly: How the Courage to Be Vulnerable Transforms the Way We Live, Love, Parent, and Lead* (Avery, 2015)

194 experience foreboding joy: ibid.

196 sharing food is even more effective: Katrien Maldoy, Charlotte J. S. De Backer and Karolien Poels, 'The pleasure of sharing: can social context make healthy

food more appealing?', *Psychology & Marketing*, 38: 2 (2021), pp. 359–70, https://onlinelibrary.wiley.com/doi/abs/10.1002/mar.21396 (accessed 16 November 2024)

198 home as a source of well-being: IKEA *Life at Home* Report 2022 (Ingka Holding B.V.)

200 the days that have passed: Meik Wiking, *The Art of Making Memories* (William Morrow, 2019)

203 'Joy is not made to be a crumb': Mary Oliver, *Devotions: The Selected Poems of Mary Oliver* (Penguin Press, 2017)

CHAPTER 8: ASPIRATION

204 '"Hope" is the thing with feathers': Emily Dickinson, '"Hope" Is the Thing with Feathers' (1891)

207 overall life satisfaction: E. L. Bradshaw, J. H. Conigrave, B. A. Steward et al., 'A meta-analysis of the dark side of the American dream: evidence for the universal wellness costs of prioritizing extrinsic over intrinsic goals', *Journal of Personality and Social Psychology*, 124: 4 (2023), pp. 873–99, https://psycnet.apa.org/doiLanding?doi=10.1037%2Fpspp0000431 (accessed 16 November 2024)

207 largest emotional gap: IKEA *Life at Home* Report 2023 (Ingka Holding B.V.)

207 'thoughts which lead to emotion': Brené Brown, *Atlas of the Heart* (Ebury Publishing, 2021)

208 The rising cost of living: IKEA *Life at Home* Report 2022 (Ingka Holding B.V.)

208 more likely to happen for men: Timothy D. Wilson, David A. Reinhard, Erin C. Westgate et al., 'Just think: the challenges of the disengaged mind', *Science*, 345: 6192 (2014), pp. 75–7, https://www.science.org/doi/10.1126/science.1250830 (accessed 16 November 2024)

210 the coming decade: 'Global Risks Report', World Economic Forum, https://www.weforum.org/publications/series/global-risks-report/ (accessed 16 November 2024)

211 worry about climate change: 'People & Planet Consumer Insights and Trends 2023', GlobeScan and Ingka Group, https://www.ingka.com/wp-content/uploads/2023/11/People-Planet-Insights-and-Trends-2023_Summary_.pdf

211 their home helps them live sustainably: IKEA *Life at Home* Report 2023 (Ingka Holding B.V.)

212 'milk packaging or garden hoses': Nick Foster, 'The Future Mundane', 7 October 2013, https://www.core77.com/posts/25678/the-future-mundane-25678# (accessed 16 November 2024)

216 interactions initiated by the user: Maxi Heitmayer, 'Screen time: why we can't stop checking our phones', London School of Economics, 15 March 2022, https://www.lse.ac.uk/research/research-for-the-world/health/screen-time-why-we-cant-stop-checking-our-phones (accessed 16 November 2024)

CONCLUSION: A NEVER-ENDING STORY

229 'When I get home': *Alice in Wonderland*, film directed by Clyde Geronimi, Wilfred Jackson and Hamilton Luske, Walt Disney Productions (1951)

235 'the caretakers for your reinventions': Colson Whitehead, *The Colossus of New York* (Doubleday, 2003)

ABOUT THE AUTHOR

Katie McCrory is a researcher and storyteller. As the Life at Home Leader at the global headquarters for IKEA in southern Sweden, since 2017 she has led the largest and most distinctive piece of international research into home: the annual IKEA Life at Home Report.

She has written and spoken extensively about life at home, ranging from media articles to longform essays and keynote talks.

Katie has lived in the UK, the US and Denmark, having moved home upward of twenty-five times. Today, she lives in Copenhagen with her husband, two young children and their enormous house cat.